WELCOME TO THE WORLD OF CROCHET

With this book, some yarn and a crochet hook, you can learn all the basic techniques of crochet in just eight hours—and then be ready to start your first project.

You can do it all by yourself, without anyone to help you. Our easy-to-follow lessons are illustrated with large, step-by-step diagrams. It's as if we're sitting there beside you giving you hints and special helps along the way.

When you feel comfortable with the basic techniques, it's time to try your hand at one of these easy projects.

TABLE OF CONTENTS

LET'S CROCHET

CHAPTER 1

Lesson 1: Getting Started 5
Lesson 2: Chain Stitch 6
Lesson 3: Working Into the Chain 9
Lesson 4: Single Crochet 10
Lesson 5: Double Crochet 12
Lesson 6: Half Double Crochet 15
Lesson 7: Treble Crochet 17
Lesson 8: Slip Stitch 20
Lesson 9: Stitch Sampler 21
Lesson 10: Bead Crochet 21
Lesson 11: Working with Colors 22
Lesson 12: Working with Thread 23
Special Helps 24
Reading Patterns 28
Gauge 29
Skill Levels 30
Standard Yarn Weight System 30
Metric Chart 31

BEGINNER RECTANGLES

CHAPTER 2

Easy Vest or Summer Top 33
Super Simple Belts 36
Simplicity Bag 38

EASY RECTANGLES

CHAPTER 3

Let's Try Lace Scarf	41
Basket-Stitch Scarf	44
Loopy Fringe Pillows	46
Layer of Luxury Comfort Afghan	48
I Love Scraps Afghan	50
Seaside Cover-Up	52

GRANNY SQUARES

CHAPTER 4

Square-Deal Shrug	56
Join-as-You-Go Scarf	61
Fantasy Afghan	63
Jazzy Diamonds	66
Baby Blocks Afghan	71

INCREASING & DECREASING

CHAPTER 5

Triangle Wrap	75
Warm Accents	77
Just for Baby	80
Colorful Table Set	85
Comfy Stripes Cardigan	87
Girl's Comfy Stripes Cardigan	91
A Touch of Red	96
Sleepy-Time Baby Blanket	100

EXTRA CREDIT

CHAPTER 6

Clusters & Stripes	103
Popcorn Diamond Pillow	105
Floral Cluster Skirt	108
Learn-To-Bead Belt	110
Beaded Party Coasters	112
Felted Catch-All Bowl	115
Felted Business Tote	117
Botanica Pillows	119
Sunshine Tote	122
Sweet William	124
Marigold	126

77

80

85

91 87

100

96

103 105 108

110 112 115

119 122 126

LET'S CROCHET

Chapter 1

LESSON 1: GETTING STARTED

To crochet, you need only a crochet hook, some yarn and a tapestry needle.

Yarn

Yarn comes in many sizes, from fine crochet cotton used for doilies, to wonderful bulky mohairs used for afghans and sweaters. The most commonly used yarn is medium (or worsted) weight. It is readily available in a wide variety of beautiful colors. This is the weight we will use in our lessons. Always read yarn labels carefully. The label will tell you how much yarn, in ounces, grams, meters and/or yards, is in the skein or ball. Read the label to find out the fiber content of the yarn, its washability, and sometimes, how to pull the yarn from the skein. Also, there is usually a dye-lot number on the label. This number assures you that the color of each skein with this number is the same. Yarn of the same color name may vary in shade somewhat from dye lot to dye lot, creating variations in color when a project is completed. Therefore, when purchasing yarn for a project, it is important to match the dye-lot numbers on the skeins.

You'll need a blunt-pointed sewing needle with an eye big enough to carry the yarn for weaving in yarn ends and sewing seams. This is a size 16 steel tapestry needle. You can buy big plastic needles called yarn needles, but they are not as good as the steel.

Hooks

Crochet hooks come in many sizes, from very fine steel hooks, used to make intricate doilies and lace, to very large ones of plastic or wood, used to make bulky sweaters or rugs.

The hooks you will use most often are made of aluminum, are about 6 inches long and are sized alphabetically by letter from B (the smallest) to K. For our lessons, you'll need a size H hook, which is a medium size.

The aluminum crochet hook looks like this:

In Fig. 1, *(A)* is the hook end, which is used to hook the yarn and draw it through other loops of yarn (called stitches). *(B)* is the throat, a shaped area that helps you slide the stitch up onto

(C) the working area. *(D)* is the fingerhold, a flattened area that helps you grip the hook comfortably, usually with your thumb and third finger; and *(E)* is the handle, which rests under your fourth and little fingers, and provides balance for easy, smooth work.

It is important that every stitch is made on the working area, never on the throat (which would make the stitch too tight) and never on the fingerhold (which would stretch the stitch).

The hook is held in the right hand, with the thumb and third finger on the fingerhold, and the index finger near the tip of the hook *(Fig. 2)*.

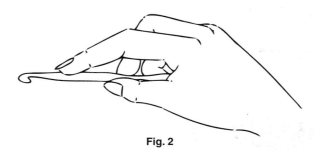

Fig. 2

The hook should be turned slightly toward you, not facing up or down. Fig. 3 shows how the hook is held, viewing from underneath the hand. The hook should be held firmly, but not tightly.

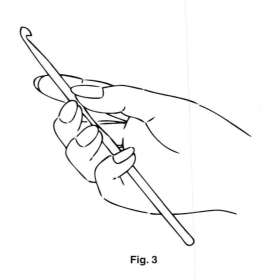

Fig. 3

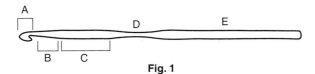

Fig. 1

LESSON 2: CHAIN STITCH
(abbreviated ch)

Crochet usually begins with a series of chain stitches called a beginning or foundation chain. Begin by making a slip knot on the hook about 6 inches from the free end of the yarn. Loop the yarn as shown in Fig. 4.

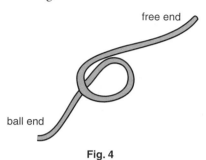

free end

ball end

Fig. 4

Insert the hook through center of loop and hook the free end *(Fig. 5)*.

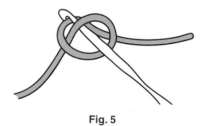

Fig. 5

Pull this through and up onto the working area of the hook *(Fig. 6)*.

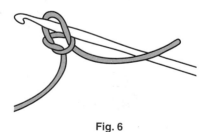

Fig. 6

Pull the free yarn end to tighten the loop *(Fig. 7)*.

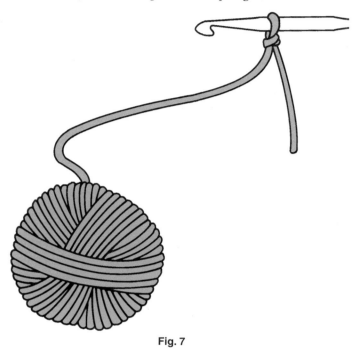

Fig. 7

It should be firm, but loose enough to slide back and forth easily on the hook. Be sure you still have about a 6-inch yarn end.

Hold the hook, now with its slip knot, in your right hand *(Fig. 8)*.

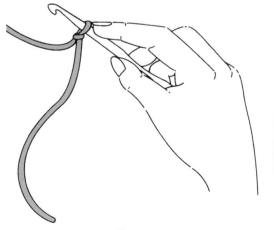

Fig. 8

Now let's make the first chain stitch.

Step 1: Hold the base of the slip knot with the thumb and index finger of your left hand, and thread yarn from the skein over the middle finger *(Fig. 9)* and under the remaining fingers of the left hand *(Fig. 9a)*.

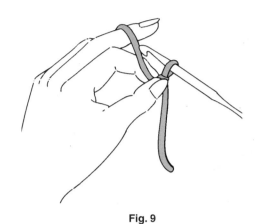

Fig. 9

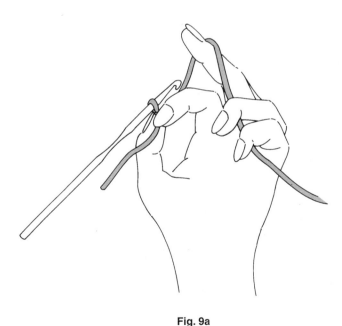

Fig. 9a

Your middle finger will stick up a bit to help the yarn feed smoothly from the skein; the other fingers help maintain even tension on the yarn as you work.

Hint: As you practice, you can adjust the way your left hand holds the thread to however is most comfortable for you.

Step 2: Bring the yarn over the hook from back to front and hook it *(Fig. 10)*.

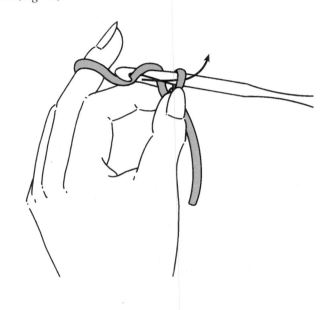

Fig. 10

Draw hooked yarn through the loop of the slip knot on the hook and up onto the working area of the hook *(see arrow on Fig. 10)*; you have now made one chain stitch *(Fig. 11)*.

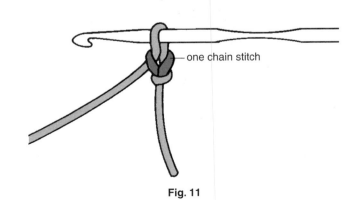

one chain stitch

Fig. 11

Step 3: Again bring the yarn over the hook from back to front *(Fig. 12a)*.

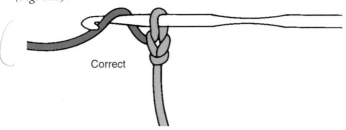

Correct

Fig. 12a

Note: Take care not to bring yarn from front to back (Fig. 12b).

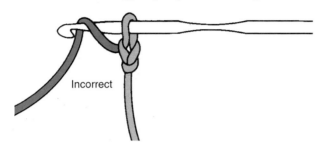

Incorrect

Fig. 12b

Hook it and draw through loop on the hook: You have made another chain stitch *(Fig. 13)*.

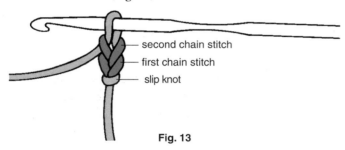

— second chain stitch
— first chain stitch
— slip knot

Fig. 13

Repeat Step 3 for each additional chain stitch, being careful to move the left thumb and index finger up the chain close to the hook after each new stitch or two *(Fig. 14a)*. This helps you control the work. *Note: Fig 14b shows the incorrect way to hold the stitches.* Also be sure to pull each new stitch up onto the working area of the hook.

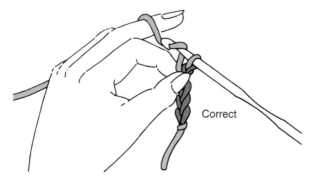

Correct

Fig. 14a

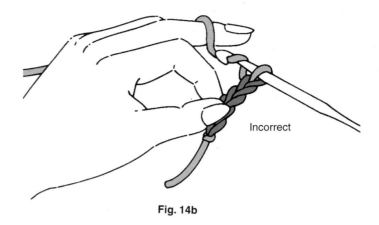

Incorrect

Fig. 14b

The working yarn and the work in progress are always held in your left hand.

Practice making chains until you are comfortable with your grip of the hook and the flow of the yarn. In the beginning your work will be uneven, with some chain stitches loose and others tight. While you're learning, try to keep the chain stitches loose. As your skill increases, the chain should be firm, but not tight, with all chain stitches even in size.

Hint: As you practice, if the hook slips out of a stitch, don't get upset! Just insert the hook again from the front into the center of the last stitch, taking care not to twist the loop *(Fig. 15)*.

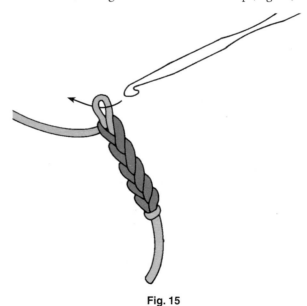

Fig. 15

When you are comfortable with the chain stitch, draw your hook out of the last stitch and pull out the work back to the beginning. Now you've learned the important first step of crochet: the beginning chain.

LESSON 3: WORKING INTO THE CHAIN

Once you have worked the beginning chain, you are ready to begin the stitches required to make any project. These stitches are worked into the foundation chain. For practice, make six chains loosely.

Hint: When counting your chain stitches at the start of a pattern—which you must do very carefully before continuing—note that the loop on the hook is never counted as a stitch, and the starting slip knot is never counted as a stitch (*Fig. 16*).

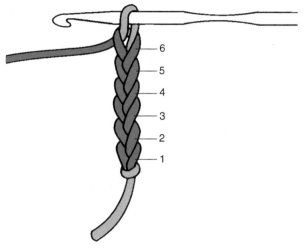

Fig. 16

Now stop and look at the chain. The front looks like a series of interlocking V's (*Fig. 16*), and each stitch has a bump or ridge at the back (*Fig. 17*).

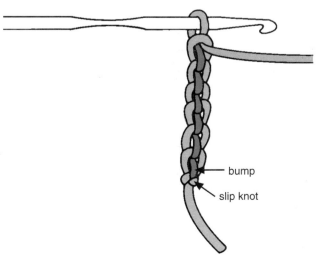

Fig. 17

You will never work into the first chain from the hook. Depending on the stitch, you will work into the second, third, fourth, etc. chain from the hook. The instructions will always state how many chains to skip before starting the first stitch.

When working a stitch, insert hook from the front of the chain, through the center of a V-stitch and under the corresponding bump on the back of the same stitch (*Fig. 18*).

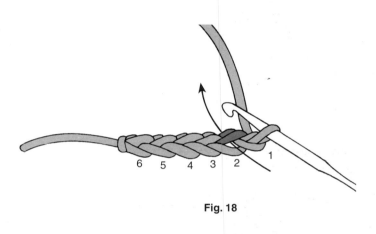

Fig. 18

Excluding the first stitch, you will work into every stitch in the chain unless the pattern states differently, but not into the starting slip knot (*Fig. 18a*). Be sure that you do not skip that last chain at the end.

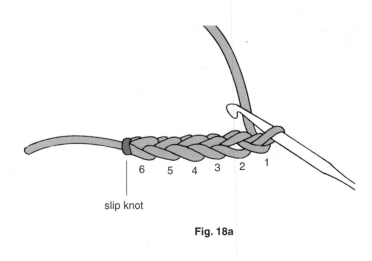

Fig. 18a

LESSON 4: SINGLE CROCHET
(abbreviated sc)

Most crochet is made with variations of just four different stitches: single crochet, double crochet, half double crochet and treble crochet. The stitches differ mainly in height, which is varied by the number of times the yarn is wrapped around the hook. The shortest and most basic of these stitches is the single crochet.

Working Row 1

To practice, begin with the chain of six stitches made in Lesson 3 and work the first row of single crochet as follows:

Step 1: Skip first chain stitch from hook. Insert hook in the second chain stitch through the center of the V and under the back bump; with third finger of your left hand, bring yarn over the hook from back to front, and hook the yarn *(Fig.19)*.

Fig. 19

Draw yarn through the chain stitch and well up onto the working area of the hook. You now have two loops on the hook *(Fig. 20)*.

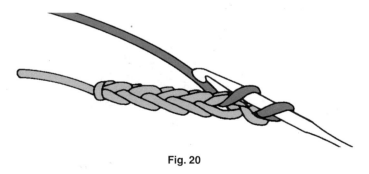

Fig. 20

Step 2: Again bring yarn over the hook from back to front, hook it and draw it through both loops on the hook *(Fig. 21)*.

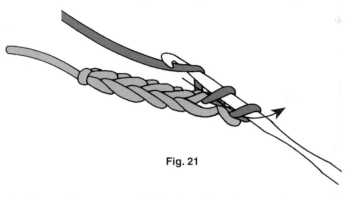

Fig. 21

One loop will remain on the hook, and you have made one single crochet *(Fig. 22)*.

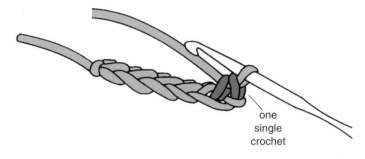

one single crochet

Fig. 22

Step 3: Insert hook in next chain stitch as before, hook the yarn and draw it through the chain stitch; hook the yarn again and draw it through both loops: You have made another single crochet.

Repeat Step 3 in each remaining chain stitch, taking care to work in the last chain stitch, **but not in the slip knot**. You have completed one row of single crochet, and should have five stitches in the row. Fig. 23 shows how to count the stitches.

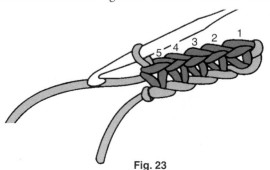

Fig. 23

American School of Needlework, Berne, IN 46711 • ASNpub.com

Hint: As you work, be careful not to twist the chain; keep all the V's facing you.

Working Row 2

To work the second row of single crochet, you need to turn the work in the direction of the arrow (counterclockwise), as shown in Fig. 24, so you can work back across the first row.

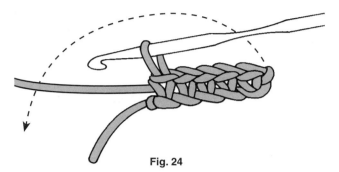

Fig. 24

Do not remove the hook from the loop as you do this (Fig. 24a).

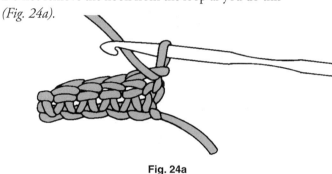

Fig. 24a

Now you need to bring the yarn up to the correct height to work the first stitch. So, to raise the yarn, chain one (this is called a turning chain).

This row, and all the following rows of single crochet, will be worked into a previous row of single crochet, not into the beginning chain as you did before. Remember that when you worked into the starting chain, you inserted the hook through the center of the V and under the bump. This is only done when working into a starting chain.

To work into a previous row of crochet, insert the hook under both loops of the previous stitch, as shown in Fig. 25, instead of through the center of the V.

Fig. 25

The first single crochet of the row is worked in the last stitch of the previous row (Fig. 25), not into the turning chain. Work a single crochet into each single crochet to the end, taking care to work in each stitch, especially the last stitch, which is easy to miss (Fig. 26).

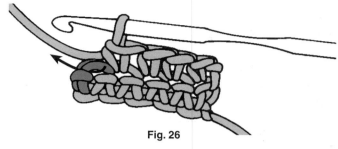

Fig. 26

Stop now and count your stitches; you should still have five single crochets on the row (Fig. 27).

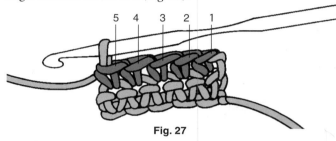

Fig. 27

Hint: When you want to pause to count stitches, check your work, have a snack or chat on the phone, you can remove your hook from the work—but do this at the end of a row, not in the middle. To remove the hook, pull straight up on the hook to make a long loop (Fig. 28). Then withdraw the hook and put it on a table or other safe place (sofas and chairs have a habit of eating crochet hooks). Put work in a safe place so loop is not pulled out. To begin work again, just insert the hook in the big loop (don't twist the loop), and pull on the yarn from the skein to tighten the loop.

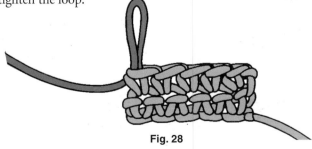

Fig. 28

To end row two, after the last single crochet, turn the work counterclockwise.

Here is the way instructions for row two might be written in a pattern:

Note: To save space, a number of abbreviations are used. For a list of abbreviations used in patterns, see page 28.

Row 2: Ch 1, sc in each sc, turn.

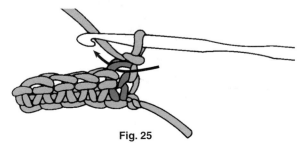

Working Row 3

Row 3 is worked exactly as you worked row 2. Here are the instructions as they would be given in a pattern:

Row 3: Rep row 2.

Now wasn't that easy? For practice, work three more rows, which means you will repeat row 2 three times more.

Hint: Try to keep your stitches as smooth and even as possible; remember to work loosely rather than tightly and to make each stitch well up on the working area of the hook. Be sure to turn at the end of each row and to check carefully to be sure you've worked into the last stitch of each row.

Count the stitches at the end of each row; do you still have five? Good work.

Hint: What if you don't have five stitches at the end of a row? Perhaps you worked two stitches in one stitch, or skipped a stitch. Find your mistake, then just pull out your stitches back to the mistake; pulling out in crochet is simple. Just take out the hook and gently pull on the yarn. The stitches will come out easily; when you reach the place where you want to start again, insert the hook in the last loop (*taking care not to twist it*) and begin.

Fastening Off

It's time to move on to another stitch, so let's fasten off your single crochet practice piece, which you can keep for future reference. After the last stitch of the last row, cut the yarn, leaving a 6-inch end. As you did when you took your hook out for a break, draw the hook straight up, but this time draw the yarn cut end completely through the stitch. Photo A shows an actual sample of six rows of single crochet to which you can compare your practice rows. It also shows how to count the stitches and rows.

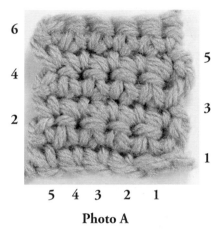

Photo A

Now you can put the piece away, and it won't pull out (*you might want to tag this piece as a sample of single crochet*).

LESSON 5: DOUBLE CROCHET
(abbreviated dc)

Double crochet is a taller stitch than single crochet. To practice, first chain 14 stitches loosely. Then work the first row of double crochet as follows:

Working Row 1

Step 1: Bring yarn once over the hook from back to front (*as though you were going to make another chain stitch*); skip the first three chains from the hook, then insert hook in the fourth chain (*Fig. 29*).

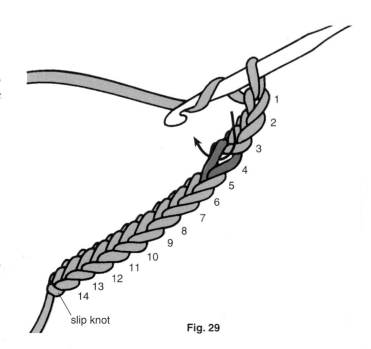

slip knot

Fig. 29

Remember not to count the loop on the hook as a chain. Be sure to go through the center of the V of the chain and under the bump at the back, and do not twist the chain.

Step 2: Hook yarn and draw it through the chain stitch and up onto the working area of the hook: you now have three loops on the hook *(Fig. 30)*.

Fig. 30

Step 3: Hook yarn and draw through the first 2 loops on the hook *(Fig. 31)*.

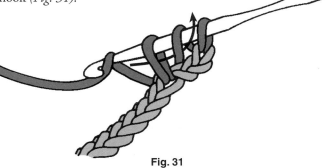

Fig. 31

You now have 2 loops on the hook *(Fig. 32)*.

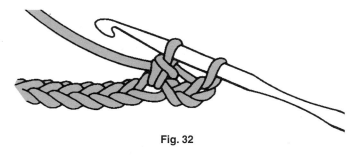

Fig. 32

Step 4: Hook yarn and draw through both loops on the hook *(Fig. 33)*.

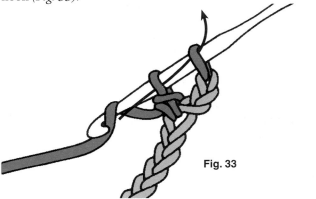

Fig. 33

You have now completed one double crochet and one loop remains on the hook *(Fig. 34)*.

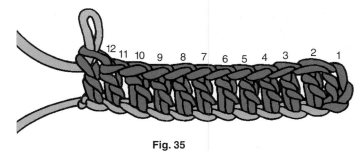

one double crochet

Fig. 34

Repeat Steps 1 through 4 in each chain stitch across *(except in Step 1, work in next chain; don't skip three chains)*.

When you've worked a double crochet in the last chain, pull out your hook and look at your work. Then count your double crochet stitches: There should be 12 of them, counting the first three chain stitches you skipped at the beginning of the row as a double crochet *(Fig. 35)*.

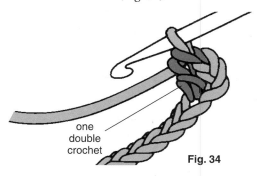

Fig. 35

Hint: In working double crochet on a beginning chain row, the three chains skipped before making the first double crochet are always counted as a double crochet stitch.

Turn the work counterclockwise before beginning row 2.

Working Row 2
To work row 2, you need to bring the thread up to the correct height for the next row. To raise the yarn, chain three *(this is called the turning chain)*.

The three chains in the turning chain just made count as the first double crochet of the new row, so skip the first double crochet and work a double crochet in the second stitch. Be sure to insert hook under top two loops of stitch: Figs. 36a and 36b indicate the correct and incorrect placement of this stitch.

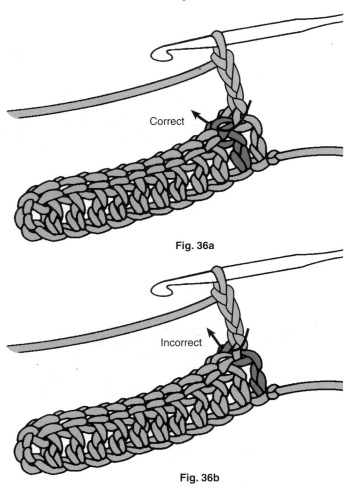

Fig. 36a

Fig. 36b

Work a double crochet in each remaining stitch across the previous row; at the end of each row, be sure to work the last double crochet in the top of the turning chain from the previous row. Be sure to insert hook in the center of the V (and back bump) of the top chain of the turning chain (*Fig. 37*). Stop and count your double crochets; there should be 12 stitches. Now, turn.

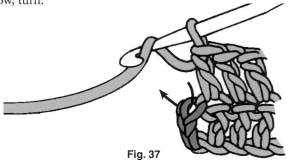

Fig. 37

Here is the way the instructions might be written in a pattern:

Row 2: Ch 3, dc in each dc, turn. *(12 dc)*

Working Row 3

Row 3 is worked exactly as you worked row 2.

In a pattern, instructions would read:

Row 3: Rep row 2.

For practice, work three more rows, repeating row 2. At the end of the last row, fasten off the yarn as you did for the single crochet practice piece. Photo B shows a sample of six rows of double crochet and how to count the stitches and rows.

Photo B

Break Time!

Now you have learned the two most-often-used stitches in crochet. Since you've worked so hard, it's time to take a break. Walk around, relax your hands, have a snack or just take a few minutes to release the stress that sometimes develops when learning something new.

LESSON 6: HALF DOUBLE CROCHET (abbreviated hdc)

Just as its name implies, this stitch eliminates one step of double crochet and works up about half as tall.

To practice, chain 13 stitches loosely.

Working Row 1

Step 1: Bring yarn once over hook from back to front, skip the first two chains, then insert hook in the third chain from the hook *(Fig. 38)*.

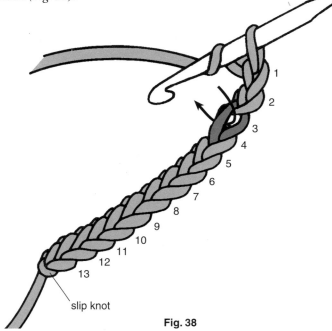

Fig. 38

Remember not to count the loop on the hook as a chain.

Step 2: Hook yarn and draw it through the chain stitch and up onto the working area of the hook. You now have three loops on the hook *(Fig. 39)*.

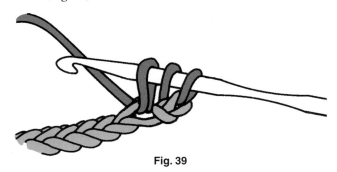

Fig. 39

Step 3: Hook yarn and draw it through all three loops on the hook in one motion *(Fig. 40)*.

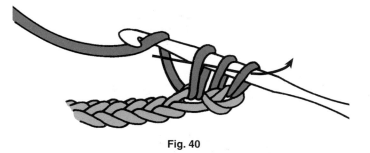

Fig. 40

You have completed one half double crochet and one loop remains on the hook *(Fig. 41)*.

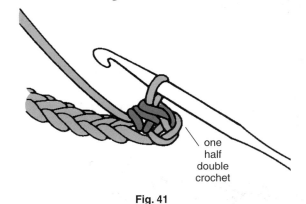

Fig. 41

In next chain stitch, work a half double crochet as follows:

Step 1: Bring yarn once over hook from back to front, insert hook in next chain.

Step 2: Hook yarn and draw it through the chain stitch and up onto the working area of the hook. You now have three loops on the hook.

Step 3: Hook yarn and draw it through all three loops on the hook in one motion.

Repeat the previous three steps in each remaining chain stitch across. Stop and count your stitches: You should have 12 half double crochets, counting the first two chains you skipped at the beginning of the row as a half double crochet *(Fig. 42)*.

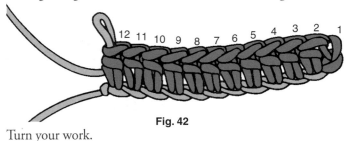

Fig. 42

Turn your work.

Working Row 2

Like double crochet, the turning chain counts as a stitch in half double crochet (unless your pattern specifies otherwise). Chain two, skip the first half double crochet of the previous row and work a half double crochet in the second stitch *(Fig. 43)* and in each remaining stitch across the previous row. At the end of the row, chain two and turn.

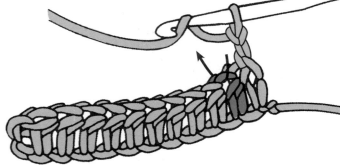

Fig. 43

Here is the way the instructions might be written in a pattern:

Row 2: Ch 2, hdc in each hdc, turn. *(12 hdc)*

Working Row 3

Row 3 is worked exactly as you worked row 2.

For practice, work three more rows, repeating row 2. Be sure to count your stitches carefully at the end of each row. When the practice rows are completed, fasten off. Photo C shows a sample of six rows of half double crochet and how to count the stitches and the rows. Continue with the next lesson.

Photo C

LESSON 7: TREBLE CROCHET
(abbreviated tr)

Treble crochet is a tall stitch that works up quickly and is fun to do. To practice, first chain 15 stitches loosely. Then work the first row as follows:

Working Row 1
Step 1: Bring yarn twice over the hook (from back to front), skip the first four chains, then insert hook into the fifth chain from the hook *(Fig. 44)*.

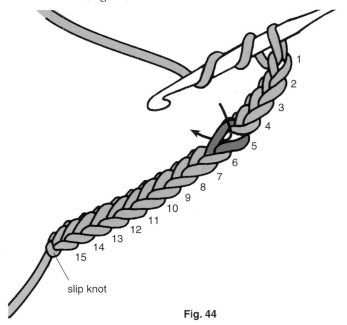

Fig. 44

Step 2: Hook yarn and draw it through the chain stitch and up onto the working area of the hook; you now have four loops on the hook *(Fig. 45)*.

Fig. 45

Step 3: Hook yarn and draw it through the first two loops on the hook *(Fig. 46)*.

Fig. 46

You now have three loops on the hook *(Fig. 46a)*.

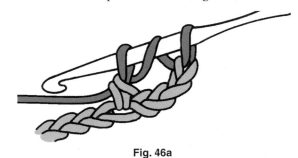

Fig. 46a

Step 4: Hook yarn again and draw it through the next two loops on the hook *(Fig. 47)*.

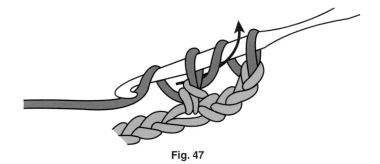

Fig. 47

Two loops remain on the hook *(Fig. 47a)*.

Fig. 47a

Step 5: Hook yarn and draw it through both remaining loops on the hook *(Fig 48)*.

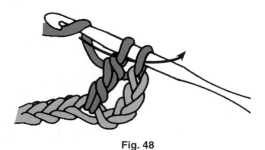

Fig. 48

You have now completed one treble crochet and one loop remains on the hook *(Fig. 49)*.

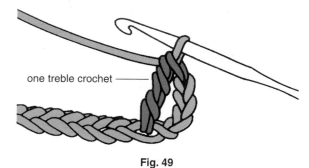

one treble crochet

Fig. 49

In next chain stitch work a treble crochet as follows:

Step 1: Bring yarn twice over the hook (from back to front); insert hook in the next chain *(Fig. 50)*.

Fig. 50

Step 2: Hook yarn and draw it through the chain stitch and up onto the working area of the hook; you now have four loops on the hook.

Step 3: Hook yarn and draw it through the first two loops on the hook.

You now have three loops on the hook.

Step 4: Hook yarn again and draw it through the next two loops on the hook.

Two loops remain on the hook.

Step 5: Hook yarn and draw it through both remaining loops on the hook.

Repeat the previous five steps in each remaining chain stitch across.

When you've worked a treble crochet in the last chain, count your stitches: There should be 12 of them, counting the first four chains you skipped at the beginning of the row as a treble crochet *(Fig. 51)*; turn work.

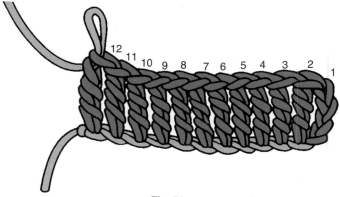

Fig. 51

American School of Needlework, Berne, IN 46711 • ASNpub.com

Hint: In working the first row of treble crochet, the four chains skipped before making the first treble crochet are always counted as a treble crochet stitch.

Working Row 2

Chain four to bring your yarn up to the correct height, and to count as the first stitch of the row. Skip the first stitch and work a treble crochet in the second stitch *(Fig. 52)*.

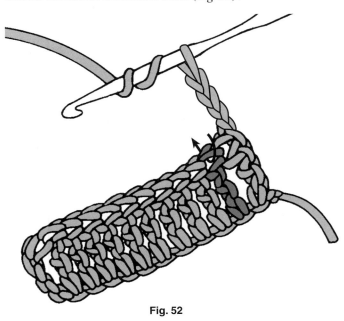

Fig. 52

Work a treble crochet in each remaining stitch across previous row; be sure to work last treble crochet in the top of the turning chain from the previous row. Count stitches: Be sure you still have 12 stitches; turn work.

Hint: Remember to work last treble crochet of each row in turning chain of previous row. Missing this stitch in the turning chain is a common error.

Here is the way the instructions might be written in a pattern:

Row 2: Ch 4, tr in each tr, turn. *(12 tr)*

Working Row 3

Work row 3 exactly as you worked row 2.

For practice, work three more rows, repeating row 2. At the end of the last row, fasten off the yarn. Photo D shows a sample of six rows of treble crochet and how to count the stitches and rows.

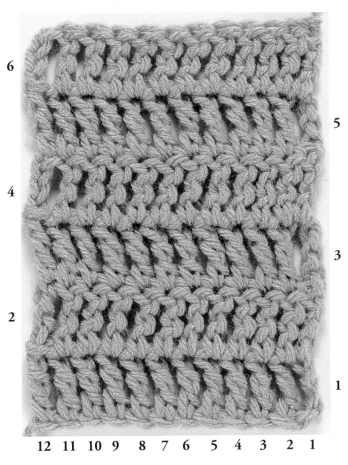

Photo D

LESSON 8: SLIP STITCH
(abbreviated sl st)

This is the shortest of all crochet stitches and is really more a technique than a stitch. Slip stitches are usually used to move yarn across a group of stitches without adding height, or they may be used to join work.

Moving Yarn Across Stitches
Chain 10.

Working Row 1
Double crochet in the fourth chain from hook *(see page 9)* and in each chain across. Turn work. On the next row, you are going to slip stitch across the first four stitches before beginning to work double crochet again.

Working Row 2
Instead of making three chains for the turning chain as you would usually do for a second row of double crochet, this time just chain one. The turning chain-one does not count as a stitch; therefore, insert hook under both loops of first stitch, hook yarn and draw it through both loops of stitch and loop on the hook *(Fig 53)*: one slip stitch made.

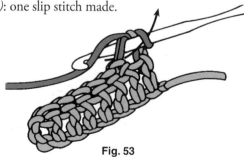

Fig. 53

Work a slip stitch in the same manner in each of the next three stitches. Now we're going to finish the row in double crochet; chain three to get yarn at the right height (the chain three counts as a double crochet), then work a double crochet in each of the remaining stitches. Look at your work and see how we moved the thread across with slip stitches, adding very little height *(Fig. 54)*.

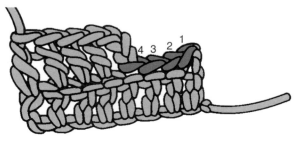

Fig. 54

Fasten off and save the sample.

Here is the way the instructions might be written in a pattern.

Row 2: Sl st in next 4 dc; ch 3, dc in each rem dc. *(5 dc)*

Fasten off.

Hint: When slip stitching across stitches, always work very loosely.

Joining Stitches

Joining a chain into a circle.
Chain six, then insert hook through the first chain you made *(next to the slip knot—Fig. 55).*

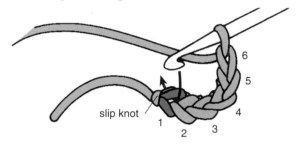

Fig. 55

Hook yarn and draw it through the chain and through the loop on hook; you have now joined the six chains into a circle or a ring. This is the way many motifs, such as granny squares, are started. Cut yarn and keep this practice piece as a sample.

Joining the end of a round to the beginning of the same round.
Chain six; join with a slip stitch in first chain you made to form a ring. Chain three; work 11 double crochet in the ring; insert hook in third chain of beginning chain three *(Fig. 56);* hook yarn and draw it through the chain and through the loop on the hook; you have now joined the round. Cut yarn and keep this piece as a sample.

Here is the way the instructions might be written in a pattern:

Rnd 1: Ch 3, 11 dc in ring; join in 3rd ch of beg ch-3.

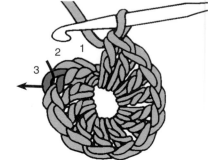

Fig. 56

LESSON 9: STITCH SAMPLER

Now you've learned the basic stitches of crochet—and wasn't it fun? The hard part is over!

To help you understand the difference in the way single crochet, half double crochet, double crochet and treble crochet stitches are worked, and the difference in their heights, let's make one more sample.

Chain 17 stitches loosely. Taking care not to work too tightly, single crochet in the second chain from hook and in each of the next three chains; work a half double crochet in each of the next four chains; work a double crochet in each of the next four chains; work a treble crochet in each of the next four chains; fasten off. Your work should look like Photo E.

Photo E

LESSON 10: BEAD CROCHET

Now that you have mastered the basic crochet stitches, it is time to learn a technique which will give your work some sparkle.

Bead crochet is a simple technique in which you add beads to your work as you crochet the stitches.

In a pattern, you will be given the size of beads necessary for the project.

Before beginning the project, slide the beads on the yarn. Follow the pattern until you are instructed to add a bead. To add a bead, simply slide a bead up to the loop on the hook *(Fig. 57)*. Now work the next stitch. Depending on which side of the work you want the bead to be, you will work the next stitch either behind the bead, to have the bead on the side of your work facing you, or by working in front of the bead, to have the bead on the side away from you.

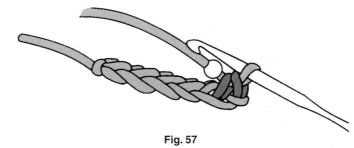

Fig. 57

LESSON 11: WORKING WITH COLORS

Working with colors often involves reading charts, changing colors, and learning how to carry or pick up colors.

Working From Charts

Charts are easy to work from once you understand how to follow them. When working from a chart, remember that for each odd-numbered row, you will work the chart from right to left, and for each even-numbered row, you will work the chart from left to right.

Odd-numbered rows are worked on the right side of the piece and even-numbered rows are worked on the wrong side. To help follow across the row, you will find it helpful to place a ruler or sheet of paper directly below the row being worked.

Changing Colors

To change from working color to a new color, work the last stitch to be done in the working color until two loops remain on the hook (Photo A). Draw new color through the two loops on hook. Drop working color (Photo B) and continue to work in the new color. This method can be used when change of color is at the end of a row or within the row.

Photo B

Carrying Or Picking Up Colors

In some patterns, you may need to carry a color on the wrong side of the work for several stitches or pickup a color used on the previous row. To carry a color means to carry the strand on the wrong side of the work. To prevent having loops of unworked yarn, it is helpful to work over the strand of the carried color. To do this, consider the strand a part of the stitch being worked into and simply insert the hook in the stitch and draw the new color through (Photo C). When changing from working color to a color that has been carried or used on the previous row, always bring this color under the working color. This is very important, as it prevents holes in your work.

Photo A

Photo C

LESSON 12: WORKING WITH THREAD

To work with thread, you will need a steel hook and some crochet thread.

Thread

Thread comes in many sizes: from very fine crochet cotton (sizes 80 and 100), used for lace-making and tatting, to sizes 30, 20 and 10, used for doilies and bedspreads. The larger the number, the thinner the thread. The most commonly used thread is size 10, and it is often called bedspread-weight. It is readily available in white, ecru and cream, as well as a wide variety of colors. As with yarn labels, always read thread labels carefully. The label will tell you how much thread is in the skein or ball in ounces, grams, meters or yards; the type of thread, usually cotton; and its washability. Also, there is usually a dye-lot number. This number assures you that the color of each ball with this number is the same. Thread with the same color name may vary from dye lot to dye lot, creating variations in color when a project is completed. Therefore, when purchasing thread for a project, it is important to match the dye-lot number on the balls.

To weave in thread ends, a size 18 steel tapestry needle works fine.

Hooks

Steel hooks are sized numerically from 14 (the smallest) to 0, and are about 5 inches long, which is shorter than aluminum or plastic hooks. Their shape is different from other crochet hooks. There is the throat, then the shank, and after the shank, the steel begins to widen again before it reaches the fingerhold *(Fig. 58)*.

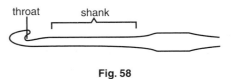

throat   shank

Fig. 58

When crocheting, it is important that the stitches do not slide beyond the shank as this will cause a loose tension and alter the gauge. If you find you are having difficulty at first, place a piece of tape around the hook to keep the stitches from sliding past the correct area. With practice, you will work in the right place automatically.

SPECIAL HELPS

Increasing & Decreasing

Shaping is done by increasing, which adds stitches to make the crocheted piece wider, or decreasing, which subtracts stitches to make the piece narrower.

Note: *Make a practice sample by chaining 15 stitches loosely and working four rows of single crochet with 14 stitches in each row. Do not fasten off at end of last row. Use this sample swatch to practice the following method of increasing stitches.*

Increasing: To increase one stitch in single, half double, double or treble crochet, simply work two stitches in one stitch. For example, if you are working in single crochet and you need to increase one stitch, you would work one single crochet in the next stitch; then you would work another single crochet in the same stitch.

For practice: On sample swatch, turn work and chain one. Single crochet in first two stitches; increase in next stitch by working two single crochets in stitch *(Fig. 59)*.

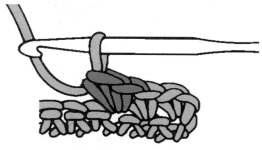

single crochet increase

Fig. 59

Repeat increase in each stitch across row to last two stitches; single crochet in each of next two stitches. Count your stitches: You should have 24 stitches. If you don't have 24 stitches, examine your swatch to see if you have increased in each specified stitch. Rework the row if necessary.

Increases in half double, double and treble crochet are shown in Figs. 59a, 59b and 59c.

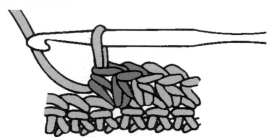

half double crochet increase

Fig. 59a

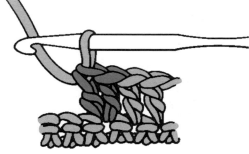

double crochet increase

Fig. 59b

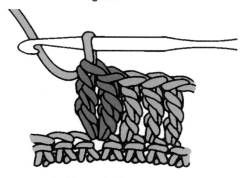

treble crochet increase

Fig. 59c

Note: *Make another practice sample by chaining 15 loosely and working four rows of single crochet. Do not fasten off at end of last row. Use this sample swatch to practice the following methods of decreasing stitches.*

Decreasing: This is how to work a decrease in the four main stitches. Each decrease gives one fewer stitch than you had before.

Single crochet decrease (sc dec): Insert hook and draw up a loop in each of the next two stitches *(three loops now on hook)*, hook yarn and draw through all three loops on the hook *(Fig. 60)*.

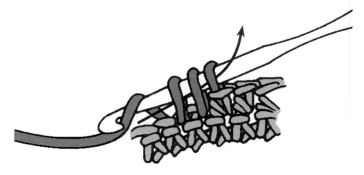

Fig. 60

Single crochet decrease made *(Fig. 61)*.

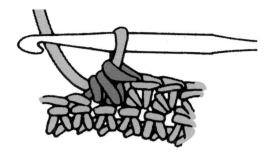

Fig. 61

Double crochet decrease (dc dec): Work a double crochet in the specified stitch until two loops remain on the hook *(Fig. 62)*.

Fig. 62

Keeping these two loops on hook, work another double crochet in the next stitch until three loops remain on hook; hook yarn and draw through all three loops on the hook *(Fig. 63)*.

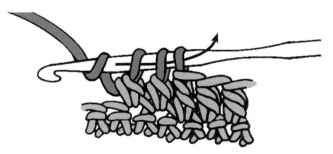

Fig. 63

Double crochet decrease made *(Fig. 64)*.

Fig. 64

Half double crochet decrease (hdc dec): Yo, insert hook in specified stitch and draw up a loop: three loops on the hook *(Fig. 65)*.

Fig. 65

Keeping these three loops on hook, yo and draw up a loop in the next stitch *(five loops now on hook)*, hook yarn and draw through all five loops on the hook *(Fig. 66)*.

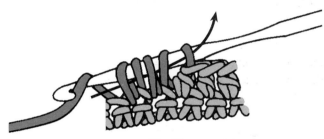

Fig. 66

Half double crochet decrease made *(Fig. 67)*.

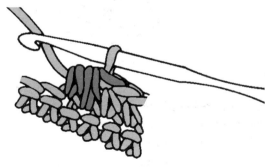

Fig. 67

Treble crochet decrease (tr dec): Work a treble crochet in the specified stitch until two loops remain on the hook *(Fig. 68)*.

Fig. 68

Keeping these two loops on hook, work another triple crochet in the next stitch until 3 loops remain on the hook; hook yarn and draw through all three loops on the hook *(Fig. 69)*.

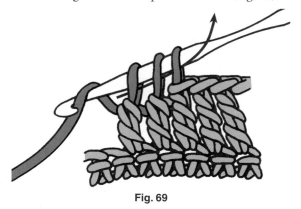

Fig. 69

Treble crochet decrease made *(Fig. 70)*.

Fig. 70

Joining New Thread

Never tie or leave knots! In crochet, yarn ends can be easily worked in and hidden because of the density of the stitches. Always leave at least 6-inch ends when fastening off yarn just used and when joining new yarn. If a flaw or a knot appears in the yarn while you are working from a skein, cut out the imperfection and rejoin the yarn.

Whenever possible, join new yarn at the end of a row. To do this, work the last stitch with the old yarn until two loops remain on the hook, then with the new yarn complete the stitch *(Fig. 71)*.

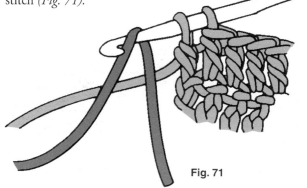

Fig. 71

To join new yarn in the middle of a row, when about 12 inches of the old yarn remains, work several more stitches with the old yarn, working the stitches over the end of new yarn *(Fig. 72 shown in double crochet)*. Then change yarns in stitch as previously explained.

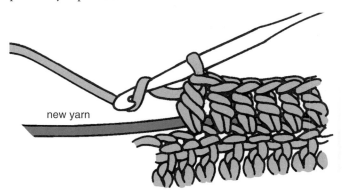

new yarn

Fig. 72

Continuing with the new yarn, work the following stitches over the old yarn end.

Finishing

A carefully crocheted project can be disappointing if the finishing has been done incorrectly. Correct finishing techniques are not difficult, but do require time, attention and a knowledge of basic techniques.

Weaving in ends: The first procedure of finishing is to securely weave in all yarn ends. Thread a size 16 steel tapestry needle with yarn, then weave running stitches either horizontally or vertically on the wrong side of work. First weave about 1 inch in one direction and then ½ inch in the reverse direction. Be sure yarn doesn't show on right side of work. Cut off excess yarn. Never weave in more than one yarn end at a time.

Sewing seams: Edges in crochet are usually butted together for seaming instead of layered, to avoid bulk. Do not sew too tightly—seams should be elastic and have the same stretch as the crocheted pieces.

Carefully matching stitches and rows as much as possible, sew the seams with the same yarn you used when crocheting.

1. Invisible seam: This seam provides a smooth, neat appearance because the edges are woven together invisibly from the right side. Join vertical edges, such as side or sleeve seams, through the matching edge stitches, bringing the yarn up through the posts of the stitches *(Fig. 73)*.

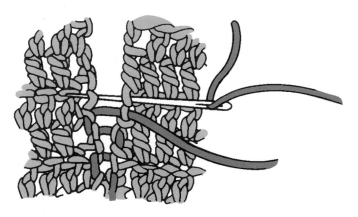

Fig. 73

If a firmer seam is desired, weave the edges together through both the tops and the posts of the matching edge stitches.

2. Backstitch seam: This method gives a strong, firm edge and is used when the seam will have a lot of stress or pull on it. Hold the pieces with right sides together and then sew through both thicknesses as shown (*Fig. 74*).

Fig. 74

3. Overcast seam: Strips and pieces of afghans are frequently joined in this manner. Hold the pieces with right sides together and overcast edges, carefully matching stitches on the two pieces (*Fig. 75*).

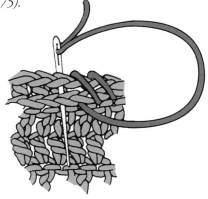

Fig. 75

Edges can also be joined in this manner, using only the back loops or the front loops of each stitch (*see page 28*).

4. Crocheted Seam: Holding pieces with right sides together, join yarn with a slip stitch at right-side edge. Loosely slip stitch

pieces together, being sure not to pull stitches too tightly (*Fig. 76*). You may wish to use a hook one size larger than the one used in the project.

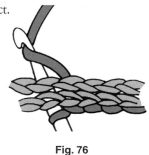

Fig. 76

Edging

Single crochet edging: A row of single crochet worked around a competed project gives a finished look. The instructions will say to "work a row of single crochet, taking care to keep work flat." This means you need to adjust your stitches as you work. To work the edging, insert hook from front to back through the edge stitch and work a single crochet. Continue evenly along the edge. You may need to skip a row or a stitch here or there to keep the edging from rippling, or add a stitch to keep the work from pulling.

When working around a corner, it is usually necessary to work at least three stitches in the corner center stitch to keep the corner flat and square (*Fig. 77*).

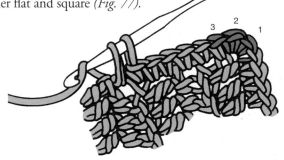

Fig. 77

Reverse single crochet edging: A single crochet edging is sometimes worked from left to right for a more dominant edge. To work reverse single crochet, insert hook in stitch to the right (*Fig. 78*), hook yarn and draw through stitch, hook yarn and draw through both loops on the hook (*Fig. 79*).

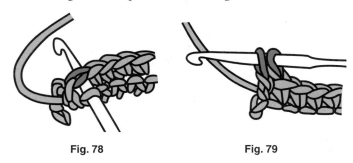

Fig. 78   **Fig. 79**

READING PATTERNS
(abbreviations, symbols and terms)

Crochet patterns are written in a special language full of abbreviations, asterisks, parentheses, brackets and other symbols and terms. These short forms are used so instructions will not take up too much space. They may seem confusing at first, but once understood, they are really easy to follow.

Abbreviations

beg	begin/beginning	fptr	front post treble crochet
bpdc	back post double crochet	g	gram(s)
bpsc	back post single crochet	hdc	half double crochet
bptr	back post treble crochet	inc	increase/increases/increasing
CC	contrasting color	lp(s)	loops(s)
ch	chain stitch	MC	main color
ch-	refers to chain or space previously made (i.e. ch-1 space)	mm	millimeter(s)
		oz	ounce(s)
		pc	popcorn
ch sp	chain space	rem	remain/remaining
cl(s)	cluster(s)	rep	repeat(s)
cm	centimeter(s)	rnd(s)	round(s)
dc	double crochet	RS	right side
dec	decrease/decreases/decreasing	sc	single crochet
		sk	skip/skipped
dtr	double treble crochet	sl st	slip stitch
		sp(s)	space(s)
Fig	figure	st(s)	stitch(es)
fpdc	front post double crochet	tog	together
		tr	treble crochet
		trtr	triple treble crochet
fpsc	front post single crochet	WS	wrong side
		yd(s)	yard(s)
		yo	yarn over

Symbols

* An asterisk is used to mark the beginning of a portion of instructions which will be worked more than once; thus, "rep from * twice" means after working the instructions once, repeat the instructions following the asterisk twice more *(3 times in all)*.

[ ] Brackets are used to enclose instructions which should be repeated the number of times specified immediately following the brackets: "[2 sc in next dc, sc in next dc] twice." Brackets

are also used to indicate additional or clarifying information for mulitple sizes: "child's size 2 [4, 6]"; "Row 29 [31, 33]."

( ) Parentheses are used to set off and clarify a group of stitches that are to be worked all into the same space or stitch, such as: "in corner sp work (2 dc, ch 1, 2 dc)."

{ } Braces are used to indicate a set of repeat instructions within a bracketed or parenthetical set of repeat instructions: "[{ch 5, sc in next sh sp} twice, ch 5, sk next dc]"; "({dc, ch 1} 5 times, dc) in next ch sp)."

Terms

Front loop (front lp) is the loop toward you at the top of the stitch *(Fig. 80)*.

Back loop (back lp) is the loop away from you at the top of the stitch *(Fig. 80)*.

Post is the vertical part of the stitch *(Fig. 80)*.

Work even means to continue to work in the pattern as established, without increasing or decreasing.

Wrong side (WS): the side of the work that will not show when project is in use.

Right side (RS): the side that will show.

Right-hand side: the side nearest your right hand as you are working.

Left-hand side: the side nearest your left hand as you are working.

Right front: The piece of a garment that will be worn on the right-hand side of the body.

Left front: The piece of a garment that will be worn on the left-hand side of the body.

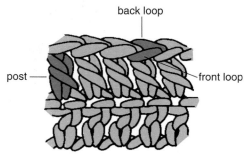

Fig. 80

GAUGE

We've left this until last, but it really is the single most important thing in crochet.

If you don't work to gauge, your crocheted projects may not be the correct size, and you may not have enough yarn to finish your project.

Gauge means the number of stitches per inch and rows per inch that result from a specified yarn worked with a specified-size hook. Since everyone crochets differently—some loosely, some tightly, some in-between—the measurements of individual work can vary greatly when using the same-size hook and yarn. It is **your responsibility** to make sure you achieve the gauge specified in the pattern.

Hook sizes given in instructions are merely guides and should never be used without making a 4-inch-square sample swatch to check gauge. Make the sample gauge swatch using the size hook, and the yarn and stitch specified in the pattern. If you have more stitches per inch than specified, try again using a larger-size hook. If you have fewer stitches per inch than specified, try again using a smaller-size hook. Do not hesitate to change to a larger- or smaller-size hook, if necessary, to achieve gauge.

If you have the correct number of stitches per inch, but cannot achieve the row gauge, adjust the height of your stitches. This means that after inserting the hook to begin a new stitch, draw up a little more yarn if your stitches are not tall enough—this makes the first loop slightly higher; or draw up less yarn if your stitches are too tall. Practice will help you achieve the correct height.

This photo shows how to measure your gauge.

SKILL LEVELS

■□□□ **BEGINNER**	Beginner projects for first-time crocheters using basic stitches. Minimal shaping.
■■□□ **EASY**	Easy projects using basic stitches, repetitive stitch patterns, simple color changes and simple shaping and finishing.
■■■□ **INTERMEDIATE**	Intermediate projects with a variety of stitches, mid-level shaping and finishing.
■■■■ **EXPERIENCED**	Experienced projects using advanced techniques and stitches, detailed shaping and refined finishing.

STANDARD YARN WEIGHT SYSTEM

Categories of yarn, gauge ranges, and recommended needle and hook sizes

Yarn Weight Symbol & Category Names	1 SUPER FINE	2 FINE	3 LIGHT	4 MEDIUM	5 BULKY	6 SUPER BULKY
Type of Yarns in Category	Sock, Fingering, Baby	Sport, Baby	DK, Light Worsted	Worsted, Afghan, Aran	Chunky, Craft, Rug	Bulky, Roving
Knit Gauge Range* in Stockinette Stitch to 4 inches	27–32 sts	23–26 sts	21–24 sts	16–20 sts	12–15 sts	6–11 sts
Recommended Needle in Metric Size Range	2.25–3.25 mm	3.25–3.75 mm	3.75–4.5 mm	4.5–5.5 mm	5.5–8 mm	8 mm and larger
Recommended Needle U.S. Size Range	1 to 3	3 to 5	5 to 7	7 to 9	9 to 11	11 and larger
Crochet Gauge* Ranges in Single Crochet to 4 inch	21–32 sts	16–20 sts	12–17 sts	11–14 sts	8–11 sts	5–9 sts
Recommended Hook in Metric Size Range	2.25–3.5 mm	3.5–4.5 mm	4.5–5.5 mm	5.5–6.5 mm	6.5–9 mm	9 mm and larger
Recommended Hook U.S. Size Range	B1–E4	E4–7	7–I9	I-9–K-10½	K-10½–M-13	M-13 and larger

* GUIDELINES ONLY: The above reflect the most commonly used gauges and needle or hook sizes for specific yarn categories.

METRIC CHART

INCHES INTO MILLIMETERS & CENTIMETERS (Rounded off slightly)

inches	mm	cm	inches	cm	inches	cm	inches	cm
1/8	3	0.3	5	12.5	21	53.5	38	96.5
1/4	6	0.6	5 1/2	14	22	56	39	99
3/8	10	1	6	15	23	58.5	40	101.5
1/2	13	1.3	7	18	24	61	41	104
5/8	15	1.5	8	20.5	25	63.5	42	106.5
3/4	20	2	9	23	26	66	43	109
7/8	22	2.2	10	25.5	27	68.5	44	112
1	25	2.5	11	28	28	71	45	114.5
1 1/4	32	3.2	12	30.5	29	73.5	46	117
1 1/2	38	3.8	13	33	30	76	47	119.5
1 3/4	45	4.5	14	35.5	31	79	48	122
2	50	5	15	38	32	81.5	49	124.5
2 1/2	65	6.5	16	40.5	33	84	50	127
3	75	7.5	17	43	34	86.5		
3 1/2	90	9	18	46	35	89		
4	100	10	19	48.5	36	91.5		
4 1/2	115	11.5	20	51	37	94		

CROCHET HOOKS CONVERSION CHART

U.S.	1/B	2/C	3/D	4/E	5/F	6/G	8/H	9/I	10/J	10½/K	N
Continental-mm	2.25	2.75	3.25	3.5	3.75	4.25	5	5.5	6	6.5	9.0

STEEL THREAD HOOKS METRIC CONVERSION CHART

U.S.	16	14	13	12	11	10	9	8	7	6	5	4	3	2	1	0	00
U.K.	-	7	6½	6	5½	5	4	3	2½	2	1½	1	1/0	2/0	3/0	00	-
Metric-mm	0.6	0.75	0.85	1.00	1.10	1.15	1.25	1.50	1.65	1.80	1.90	2.00	2.10	2.20	2.25	2.50	2.70

EASY VEST OR SUMMER TOP

Design by Darla Sims

Skill Level

EASY

Finished Sizes

Instructions given fit woman's small; changes for medium, large, X-large, 2X-large, 3X-large, 4X-large and 5X-large are in [ ].

Finished Garment Measurements

Chest: 36 *(small)* [40 *(medium)*, 44 *(large)*, 48 *(X-large)*, 52 *(2X-large)*, 56 *(3X-large)*, 60 *(4X-large)*, 64 *(5X-large)*] inches

Materials

- Aunt Lydia's Quick Crochet medium (worsted) weight yarn (400 yds per ball): 2 [2, 3, 3, 4, 5, 5, 6] balls #1007 cranberry
- Sizes F/5/3.75mm, G/6/4mm and H/8/5mm crochet hooks or size needed to obtain gauge
- Tapestry needle
- Plastic stitch markers

Gauge

With H hook: 3 dc = 1 inch
Take time to check gauge.

Pattern Note

Top is made of 2 pieces worked lengthwise. Each piece is folded in half to create 1 half of sweater, going up and over shoulders from lower edge of front to lower edge of back. Pieces are joined at center front and back to create V-neck openings.

INSTRUCTIONS

Front/Back

Make 2.

Row 1: With H hook, ch 122 [126, 126, 126, 128, 128, 132, 132]; dc in 4th ch from hook *(beg 3 sk chs count as a dc)* and in each rem ch, turn. *(120 [124, 124, 124, 126, 126, 130, 130] dc)*

Row 2: Ch 3 *(counts as a dc on this and following rows)*, dc in each dc and in 3rd ch of beg 3 sk chs, turn.

Row 3: Ch 3, dc in each dc and in 3rd ch of turning ch-3, turn.

Rep row 3 until piece measures 9 [10, 11, 12, 13, 14, 15, 16] inches.

Fasten off and weave in ends.

Assembly

Fold each piece in half and place markers to mark shoulder line (fold line). For all sizes, measure 8 inches down from shoulder line for front neck opening on both pieces. Place pieces side by side. Beg at lower front and working through **back lps** *(see page 28)* only, sew pieces tog to marker. For all sizes, place markers 6 inches down from shoulder line for back neck opening on both pieces. Beg at lower edge, sew pieces tog to marker in same manner.

Place markers 8 [8½, 8½, 8½, 9, 9, 9½, 10] inches down from shoulder on outer edges of each piece for armholes. Working through **back lps** (see page 28) only, sew side seams from lower edge to markers.

Neck Edging

With G hook, join yarn in 1 shoulder marker; ch 1, working in sts across neck edge, work 25 sc evenly spaced from shoulder to 1 st before bottom of V-neck, **sc dec** (see page 24) in next st and in next st on next edge; working across piece, work 25 sc evenly spaced to shoulder marker; working on back neck edge, work 18 sc evenly spaced to 1 st before bottom of V-neck; sc dec in next st and in next st on next edge; work 18 sc evenly spaced to first sc; join with sl st in first sc.

Fasten off and weave in ends.

Armhole Edging

Rnd 1 (RS): Hold piece with RS facing you; with F hook, join yarn in bottom of 1 armhole opening; ch 1, working in ends of rows around armhole opening, work 25 [27, 27, 27, 29, 29, 31, 33] sc evenly spaced to shoulder; work 25 [27, 27, 27, 29, 29, 31, 33] sc evenly spaced to first sc; join with sl st in first sc.

Rnd 2: Ch 1, sc in same sc and in each rem sc; join with sl st in first sc.

Rnd 3: Rep rnd 2.

Fasten off and weave in ends.

Lower Edging

Rnd 1 (RS): Hold piece with RS of Front facing you and lower edge at top; with F hook, join yarn in right-hand side seam; working in end sts of dc rows, work 30 [32, 34, 36, 38, 40, 42, 44] sc evenly spaced to center front; work 30 [32, 34, 36, 38, 40, 42, 44] evenly spaced to next side seam, work 30 [32, 34, 36, 38, 40, 42, 44] evenly spaced to center back, work 30 [32, 34, 36, 38, 40, 42, 44] sc evenly spaced to first sc; join with sl st in

first sc. (120 [128, 136, 144, 152, 160, 168, 176] sc)

Rnd 2: Ch 1, sc in same sc and in next sc; *sc dec in next 2 sc; sc in next 2 sc; rep from * to last 2 sc; sc dec in last 2 sc; join with sl st in first sc. (90 [96, 102, 108, 114, 120, 126, 132] sc)

Rnd 3: Ch 1, sc in same sc and in each rem sc; join with sl st in first sc.

Rnds 4 & 5: Rep rnd 3.

Fasten off and weave in ends.

SUPER SIMPLE BELTS

Design by Katherine Eng

Skill Level

EASY

Finished Sizes

Tied Version: approximately
1¾ x 46½ inches
Belted Version: approximately
1¾ x 40 inches

Materials

- TLC Cotton Plus medium (worsted) weight cotton yarn (solids: 3½ oz/178 yds/100g; multis: 3 oz/153 yds/85g per skein): 1 skein #3667 turquoise *(A)* or #3615 jazz multi *(B)*
- Size H/8/5mm crochet hook or size needed to obtain gauge
- Tapestry needle
- 2-inch craft rings (for belted version): 2

4 MEDIUM

Gauge

With 2 strands held tog: 4 sc = 1½ inches

INSTRUCTIONS

Tied Version

Note: Belt is worked with 2 strands held tog.

Row 1 (RS): With A, ch 7; sc in 2nd ch from hook and in each rem ch, turn. *(6 sc)*

Row 2: Ch 1, sc in each sc, turn.

Rows 3–148: Rep row 2.

Row 149: Ch 1, **sc dec** *(see page 24)* in first 2 sc; in next sc work (sc, hdc), ch 2, in next sc work (hdc, sc); sc dec in next 2 sc. Do not turn.

Edging

Ch 2, working across side in ends of rows, sl st in end of row 148; *ch 2, sk next row, sl st in next row; rep from * to row 1; ch 1, sk row 1, working across next side in unused lps of beg ch, sc dec in first 2 lps; in next lp work (sc, hdc); in next sc work (hdc, sc); sc dec in last 2 lps; ch 2, working across next side in ends of rows, sl st in end of row 2; **ch 2, sk next row, sl st in next row; rep from ** to row 148; ch 2, sk row 148; join in first st of row 149.

Fasten off and weave in ends.

Belted Version

Note: Belt is worked with 2 strands held tog.

Row 1 (RS): With B, ch 7; sc in 2nd ch from hook and in each rem ch, turn. *(6 sc)*

Row 2: Ch 1, sc in each sc, turn.

Rows 3–178: Rep row 2.

Row 179: Ch 1, **sc dec** *(see page 24)* in first 2 sc; in next sc work (sc, hdc), ch 2, in next sc work (hdc, sc); sc dec in next 2 sc. Do not turn. Mark this end for sewing over rings.

Edging

Ch 2, working across side in ends of rows, sl st in end of row 178; *ch 2, sk next row, sl st in next row; rep from * to row 1; ch 1, sk row 1, working across next side in unused lps of beg ch, sc dec in first 2 lps; in next lp work (sc, hdc); in next sc work (hdc, sc); sc dec in last 2 lps; ch 2, working across next side in ends of rows, sl st in end of row 2; **ch 2, sk next row, sl st in next row; rep from ** to row 178; ch 2, sk row 178; join in first st of row 179.

Fasten off and weave in ends.

Finishing

Sew marked end over 2 craft rings.

SIMPLICITY BAG

Design by Darla Sims

Skill Level

EASY

Finished Size

Approximately 16 x 10½ inches

Materials

- Red Heart Casual Cot'n Blend bulky (chunky) weight yarn (4 oz/140 yds/113g per ball): 2 ball #3217 creamy *(A)* 1 ball #3427 preppie *(B)*
- TLC Cotton Plus medium (worsted) weight yarn (3½ oz/178 yds/100g per ball): 10 yds #3707 medium rose *(C)*
- Size I/9/5.5mm crochet hook or size needed to obtain gauge
- Tapestry needle
- 1 pair pink acrylic purse handles
- 8 white 6mm pearls
- 2 white 8mm pearls
- Sewing needle and matching thread

Gauge

5 sts = 2 inches

INSTRUCTIONS

Bag

Row 1 (RS): With A, ch 42; dc in 4th ch from hook *(beg 3 sk chs count as a dc)* and in each rem ch, turn. *(40 dc)*

Row 2: Ch 3 *(counts as a dc on this and following rows)*, dc in each rem dc and in 3rd ch of beg 3 sk chs, turn.

Row 3: Ch 3, dc in each rem dc and in 3rd ch of turning ch-3, turn.

Rows 4–9: Rep row 3.

Row 10: Ch 3, dc in each rem dc and in 3rd ch of turning ch-3; change to B by drawing lp through; cut C, turn.

Rows 11–19: Rep row 3.

Row 20: Ch 3, dc in each rem dc and in 3rd ch of turning ch-3; change to A by drawing lp through; cut B, turn.

Rows 21–29: Rep row 3.

Row 30: Ch 3, dc in each rem dc and in 3rd ch of turning ch-3.

Fasten off and weave in ends.

Assembly

Make 4 small 1-inch pleats across each end of piece. With tapestry needle and A, sew pleats in place.

Fold piece in half with RS tog. Sew side seams, leaving top 5 rows unsewn on each side. Turn bag RS out.

Leaf
Make 8.

With B, ch 10; sl st in 2nd ch from hook, sc in next 2 chs, hdc in next 3 chs, dc in last 3 chs.

Fasten off and weave in ends.

Large Flower
Make 2.

With C, *ch 10, sl st in 10th ch from hook—*petal made*; rep from * 9 times.

Fasten off and weave in ends.

Small Flower
Make 8.

With C, *ch 8, sl st in 8th ch from hook—*petal made*; rep from * 7 times.

Fasten off and weave in ends.

Finishing

Step 1: With sewing needles and matching thread, sew a 6mm pearl to center of each Small Flower and sew an 8mm pearl to center of each Large Flower.

Step 2: Referring to photo for placement, sew Leaves and Flowers to top edges of bag.

Step 3: With tapestry needle and A, sew handles to top of bag.

EASY
RECTANGLES

Chapter 3

LET'S TRY LACE SCARF

Design by Mary Ann Sipes

Skill Level

EASY

Finished Size

Approximately 35¼ x 67 inches

Materials

- Caron Simply Soft medium (worsted) weight yarn (3 oz/165 yds/84g per skein): 2 skeins #2713 buttercup
- Size H/8/5mm crochet hook or size needed to obtain gauge
- Tapestry needle

Gauge

4 sc = 1 inch

INSTRUCTIONS

Center

Row 1 (WS): Ch 20; sc in 2nd ch from hook and in each rem ch, turn. *(19 sc)*

Row 2 (RS): Ch 3 *(counts as a dc on this and following rows)*, dc in each rem sc, turn.

Row 3: Ch 1, sc in each dc and in 3rd ch of turning ch-3, turn.

Row 4: Ch 3, dc in next 7 sc, ch 1, sk next sc, dc in next sc, ch 1, sk next sc, dc in last 8 sc, turn.

Row 5: Ch 1, sc in each dc, in each ch-1 sp and in 3rd ch of turning ch-3, turn.

Row 6: Ch 3, dc in next 6 sc, ch 1, sk next 2 sc, 3 dc in next sc; ch 1, sk next 2 sc, dc in last 7 sc, turn.

Row 7: Rep row 5.

Row 8: Ch 3, dc in next 3 sc, ch 1, [sk next 2 sc, 3 dc in next sc] 3 times; ch 1, sk next 2 sc, dc in last 4 sc, turn.

Row 9: Rep row 5.

Row 10: Ch 4 *(counts as a dc and a ch-1 sp on this and following rows)*, [sk next 2 sc, 3 dc in next sc] 5 times; ch 1, sk next 2 sc, dc in last sc, turn.

Row 11: Ch 1, sc in each dc and in each ch-1 sp to turning ch-4; sc in sp formed by turning ch-4 and in 3rd ch of same turning ch-4, turn.

Row 12: Ch 3, dc in next 3 sc, ch 1, [sk next 2 sc, 3 dc in next sc] 3 times; ch 1, sk next 2 sc, dc in last 4 sc, turn.

Row 13: Rep row 5.

Row 14: Ch 3, dc in next 6 sc, ch 1, sk next 2 sc, 3 dc in next sc; ch 1, sk next 2 sc, dc in last 7 sc, turn.

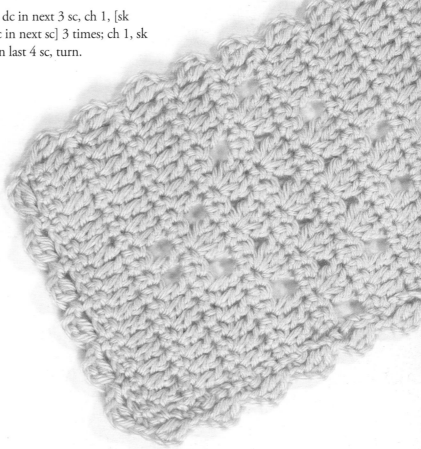

Row 15: Rep row 5.

Row 16: Ch 3, dc in next 7 sc, ch 1, sk next sc, dc in next sc, ch 1, sk next sc, dc in last 8 sc, turn.

Row 17: Rep row 5.

Row 18: Ch 3, dc in each sc, turn.

Row 19: Ch 1, sc in each dc and in 3rd ch of turning ch-3, turn.

Rows 20–163: [Work rows 4–19] 9 times.

Border

Ch 1, sc in first sc, working across last row, [ch 3, dc in 3rd ch from hook, sk next 2 sc, sc in next sc] 6 times; working across next side in ends of rows, *ch 3, dc in 3rd ch from hook, sk next dc row, sc in next sc row; rep from * across to next corner; working across next side in unused lps of beg ch, [ch 3, dc in 3rd ch from hook, sk next 2 unused lps, sc in next lp] 6 times; working across next side in ends of rows, **ch 3, dc in 3rd ch from hook, sk next dc row, sc in next sc row; rep from ** to first sc; ch 3, dc in 3rd ch from hook; join with sl st in first sc.

Fasten off and weave in ends.

BASKET-STITCH SCARF

Design by Mary Griffin

Skill Level

EASY

Finished Size

Approximately 7 x 83 inches, excluding Fringe

Materials

- Lion Brand Homespun bulky (chunky) weight yarn (6 oz/185 yds/170g per skein): 2 skeins #329 waterfall
- Size K/10½/6.5mm crochet hook or size needed to obtain gauge
- Tapestry needle

Gauge

(3 dc, ch 1) = 1 inch

INSTRUCTIONS

Row 1 (RS): Ch 20; sc in 2nd ch from hook; *ch 2, sk next 2 sc, sc in next ch, rep from * across, turn. *(6 ch-2 sps)*

Row 2: Ch 4 *(counts as a dc and a ch-1 sp on this and following rows)*, [3 dc in next ch-2 sp, ch 1] 6 times; dc in last sc, turn.

Row 3: Ch 1, sc in next ch-1 sp; *ch 2, sc in next ch-1 sp, rep from * to turning ch-4; ch 2, sc in sp formed by turning ch-4, turn.

Rep rows 2 and 3 until piece measures approximately 83 inches from beg. At end of last row, do not turn.

Fasten off and weave in ends.

Fringe

Cut 24-inch strands of yarn. For each knot of fringe use 6 strands. Fold strands in half. Draw folded end through first ch-2 sp at 1 short end of Scarf. Draw ends through fold and tighten knot. Tie knots in each rem ch-2 sp across end and in each ch-2 sp on opposite end. Trim ends even. Tie knot in each strand about 2 inches from bottom to prevent raveling.

LOOPY FRINGE PILLOWS

Design by Elaine Bartlett

Skill Level

EASY

Finished Size

Approximately 12½ x 12½ inches

Materials

- Aunt Lydia's Madison Avenue Crochet light (light worsted) weight yarn (1¾ oz/88 yds/50g per ball):
  4 balls #491 burgundy *(A)*
- Red Heart Super Saver medium (worsted) weight yarn (7 oz/364 yds/198g per skein):
  1 skein #657 dusty teal *(B)*
- Sizes H/8/5mm and I/9/5.5mm crochet hooks or size needed to obtain gauge
- Tapestry needle
- 12-inch square pillow forms: 2
- Safety pins

Gauge

With H hook: 14 sts = 4½ inches

INSTRUCTIONS

Panel

Make 2 each of A & B.

Row 1 (RS): With I hook, ch 43; change to H hook; sc in 2nd ch from hook, dc in next ch; *sc in next ch, dc in next ch; rep from * across, turn. *(42 sts)*

Row 2: Ch 1, sc in first dc, dc in next sc; *sc in next dc, dc in next sc, rep from across, turn.

Rows 3–42: Rep row 2.

Fasten off and weave in ends.

Edging

Rnd 1: Hold 2 matching Panels with WS tog, carefully matching sts; working through both thicknesses at same time, with H hook and matching yarn, make slip knot on hook and join with sc in upper right-hand corner; 2 sc in same sp; working across next side work 41 sc evenly spaced to next corner; 3 sc in corner; work across next side in ends of rows, work 41 sc evenly spaced to next corner; 3 sc in corner; working across next side in unused lps of beg ch, work 41 sc evenly spaced to next corner; 3 sc in corner; working across next side in ends of rows, work 41 sc to joining sc; join with sl st in joining sc. *(176 sc)*

Rnd 2: Change to I hook; ch 1, sc in same sc as joining; ch 10; *sc in next sc, ch 10, rep from * around; join with sl st in first sc.

Fasten off and weave in ends.

Rep Edging with 2nd set of Panels.

LAYER OF LUXURY COMFORT AFGHAN

Design by Jacqueline Stetter

Skill Level

EASY

Finished Size

Approximately 52 by 65 inches

Materials

- Medium (worsted) weight yarn: 36 oz (1800 yds, 1021g) light green *(A)* 30 oz (1500 yds, 851g) blue/green variegated *(B)*
- Size N/13/9mm crochet hook or size needed to obtain gauge
- Tapestry needle

4 MEDIUM

Gauge

With 2 strands held tog: 7 dc = 3 inches

INSTRUCTIONS

Center

Row 1 (RS): With 1 strand each A and B held tog, ch 103; dc in 3rd ch from hook *(beg 2 sk chs count as a dc)* and in each rem ch, turn.

Row 2: Ch 2 *(counts as a dc on this and following rows)*, dc in each dc, turn.

Rep row 2 until piece measures approximately 60 inches.

Fasten off and weave in all ends.

Border

Rnd 1: Hold Center with RS facing you and last row worked at top; join A with sl st in upper right-hand corner; ch 2 *(counts as a hdc on this and following rnds)*, hdc in each dc to next corner; 3 hdc in corner; hdc evenly spaced along side to next corner; 3 hdc in corner; hdc in each unused lp of beg ch to next corner; 3 hdc in corner; hdc evenly spaced along side to next corner; 2 hdc in corner; join with sl st in 2nd ch of beg ch-2.

Rnd 2: Ch 2, hdc in each hdc around, working 3 hdc in 2nd hdc of each corner, join with sl st in 2nd ch of beg ch-2.

Rnd 3: Rep rnd 2.

Rnd 4: *Ch 4, sk next hdc, sc in next hdc; rep from * around; join with sl st in first ch of beg ch-4. Fasten off.

Rnd 5: Join B with sl st in first sk hdc on rnd 3; *ch 4, working in front of ch-4 sp on rnd 4, sc in next sk hdc on rnd 3, ch 4, working in back of next ch-4 sp, sc in next sk hdc on rnd 3; rep from * around, join with sl st in joining sl st.

Fasten off and weave in all ends.

I LOVE SCRAPS AFGHAN

Design by Mary Ann Frits

Skill Level

EASY

Size

Approximately 42 x 62 inches, excluding Fringe

Materials

- Medium (worsted) weight yarn:  33½ oz/2,345 yds/ 1,005g off-white (A) 32 oz/2,240 yds/960g assorted scrap colors
- Size H/8/5mm crochet hook or size needed to obtain gauge
- Tapestry needle

Gauge

11 dc = 3 inches

Special Stitches

Shell:
In st indicated, work (2 dc, ch 1, 2 dc).

Long double crochet (long dc):
Insert hook in st indicated and draw up lp to height of working row; yo and draw through 2 lps on hook.

Pattern Note

To change colors, work until 2 loops of last stitch remain on hook. With new color, yarn over and draw through 2 loops on hook. Cut old color.

INSTRUCTIONS

Row 1 (RS): With A, ch 169; dc in 4th ch from hook *(beg 3 sk chs count as a dc)* and in each rem ch, changing to any scrap color in last dc, turn. *(167 dc)*

Row 2: Ch 3 *(counts as a dc on this and following rows)*, dc in first dc, ch 2, sk next 5 dc; *in next dc work **shell** *(see Special Stitches)*; ch 2, sk next 6 dc; rep from * 21 times; in next dc work shell; ch 2, sk next 5 dc, 2 dc in 3rd ch of beg 3 sk chs, changing to A in last dc, turn. *(23 shells)*

Row 3: Ch 1, sc in first dc, ch 1, sk next dc, working over next ch-2 sp, sk next sk dc on 2nd row below, **long dc** *(see Special Stitches)* in next 2 sk dc; *ch 2, on working row, sk next 2 dc, sc in next ch-1 sp, ch 2, sk next 2 dc, working over next ch-2 sp, sk next 2 sk dc on 2nd row below, long dc in next 2 sk dc; rep from * 22 times; ch 1, on working row, sk next dc, sc in 3rd ch of turning ch-3, turn.

Row 4: Ch 3, dc in next ch-1 sp and in next 2 dc; *2 dc in next ch-2 sp; dc in next sc, 2 dc in next ch-2 sp; dc in next 2 dc; rep from * 22 times; dc in next ch-1 sp and in next sc, changing to new scrap color in last dc, turn.

Row 5: Ch 3, dc in first dc, ch 2, sk next 5 dc; *in next dc work shell; ch 2, sk next 6 dc; rep from * 21 times; in next dc work shell; ch 2, sk next 5 dc, 2 dc in 3rd ch of turning ch-3, changing to A in last dc, turn.

Rep rows 3–5 until piece measures approximately 62 inches, ending with a row 4.

Fasten off and weave in all ends.

Fringe

Cut 25-inch strands of A. For each knot of fringe, hold 6 strands tog and fold in half. Draw folded end through first st on 1 short end of afghan. Draw ends through fold and tighten knot. Tie knots evenly spaced across each short end of afghan. Trim ends even.

SEASIDE COVER-UP

Design by Joyce Nordstrom

Skill Level

EASY

Finished Sizes

Instructions given fit woman's small; changes for medium, large, X-large, 2X-large, 3X-large, 4X-large and 5X-large are in [ ].

Finished Garment Measurements

Chest: 36 inches *(small)* [40 inches *(medium)*, 44 inches *(large)*, 48 inches *(X-large)*, 52 inches *(2X-large)*, 56 inches *(3X-large)*, 60 inches *(4X-large)*, 64 inches *(5X-large)*]

Materials

- TLC Cotton Plus medium (worsted) weight yarn (3½ oz/178 yds/100g per skein): 7 (8, 8, 9, 9, 10, 10, 11) skeins #3252 tangerine
- Size H/8/5mm crochet hook or size needed to obtain gauge
- Tapestry needle
- Stitch marker
- 5 matching ½-inch buttons
- Sewing needle and matching thread

Gauge

5 sts = 2 inches
Take time to check gauge.

INSTRUCTIONS

Back

Row 1 (RS): Ch 74 [82, 90, 98, 106, 114, 122, 130]; sc in 2nd ch from hook; *ch 1, sk next ch, sc in next ch; rep from * across, turn. *(73 [81, 89, 97, 105, 113, 121, 129] sts)*

Row 2: Ch 3 *(counts as a dc on this and following rows)*, *ch 1, sk next ch-1 sp, dc in next sc; rep from * across, turn. *(37 [41, 45, 49, 53, 57, 61, 65] dc)*

Row 3: Ch 1, sc first dc; *ch 1, sk next ch-1 sp, sc in next dc; rep from * to last ch-1 sp; ch 1, sk last ch-1 sp, sc in 3rd ch of turning ch-3, turn.

Rep rows 2 and 3 until piece measures 25 [25, 25, 26, 26, 26, 27, 27] inches from beg.

Fasten off and weave in ends.

Left Front

Row 1: Ch 38 [42, 46, 50, 54, 58, 62, 66]; sc in 2nd ch from hook; *ch 1, sk next ch, sc in next ch; rep from * across, turn. *(37 [41, 45, 49, 53, 57, 61, 65] sts)*

Row 2: Ch 3 *(counts as a dc on this and following rows)*, *ch 1, sk next ch-1 sp, dc in next sc; rep from * across, turn. *(19 [21, 23, 25, 27, 29, 31, 33] dc)*

Row 3: Ch 1, sc first dc; *ch 1, sk next ch-1 sp, sc in next dc; rep from * to last ch-1 sp; ch 1, sk last ch-1 sp, sc in 3rd ch of turning ch-3, turn.

Rep rows 2 and 3 until piece measures 21 [21, 21, 22, 22, 22, 23, 23] inches from beg, ending with a row 2.

Neck Shaping

Row 1: Ch 1, sc first dc; *ch 1, sk next ch-1 sp, sc in next dc; rep from * to last 5 [5, 5, 5, 7, 7, 9, 9] dc and turning ch-3, turn, leaving rem sts unworked.

Row 2: Ch 3, sk next ch-1 sp, dc in next sc; *ch 1, sk next ch-1 sp, dc in next sc; rep from * across, turn.

Row 3: Ch 1, sc first dc; *ch 1, sk next ch-1 sp, sc in next dc; rep from * to turning ch-3, turn, leaving turning ch-3 unworked.

Rep rows 2 and 3 until piece measures same as Back.

Fasten off and weave in ends.

Right Front

Work same as Left Front to Neck Shaping.

Neck Shaping

Row 1: Hold piece with RS facing you; sk first 6 [6, 6, 6, 8, 8, 10, 10] dc; join yarn with sl st in next dc; ch 1, sc in same dc; *ch 1, sk next ch-1 sp, sc in next dc; rep from * to last ch-1 sp; ch 1, sk last ch-1 sp, sc in 3rd ch of turning ch-3, turn.

Row 2: Ch 3 *(counts as a dc on this and following rows)*, *ch 1, sk next ch-1 sp, dc in next st; rep from * to last 2 ch-1 sps; ch 1, sk next ch-1 sp; **dc dec** *(see page 24)* in next 2 sc, turn.

American School of Needlework, Berne, IN 46711 • ASNpub.com

Row 3: Ch 1, sc in first dc; *ch 1, sk next ch-1 sp, sc in next dc; rep from * to last ch-1 sp; ch 1, sk next ch-1 sp, sc in 3rd ch of turning ch-3, turn.

Rep rows 2 and 3 until piece measures same as Back.

Fasten off and weave in ends.

Sleeve
Make 2.

Row 1 (RS): Ch 46 [46, 46, 50, 50, 54, 58, 58]; sc in 2nd ch from hook; *ch 1, sk next ch, sc in next ch; rep from * across, turn. *(45 [45, 45, 49, 49, 53, 57, 57] sts)*

Row 2: Ch 3 *(counts as a dc on this and following rows)*, *ch 1, sk next ch-1 sp, dc in next sc; rep from * across, turn.

Row 3: Ch 1, sc in first dc; *ch 1, sk next ch-1 sp, sc in next dc; rep from * to last ch-1 sp; ch 1, sk last ch-1 sp, sc in 3rd ch of turning ch-3, turn.

Row 4: Ch 4 *(counts as a dc and a ch-1 sp on this and following rows)*, dc in first sc; *ch 1, sk next ch-1 sp, dc in next sc; rep from * to last ch-1 sp; ch 1, sk last ch-1 sp, in last sc work (dc, ch 1, dc), turn. *(49 [49, 49, 53, 53, 57, 61, 61] sts)*

Row 5: Ch 1, sc in first dc; *ch 1, sk next ch-1 sp, sc in next dc; rep from * to turning ch-4; ch 1, sc in 3rd ch of turning ch-4, turn.

Row 6: Ch 4, dc in first sc; *ch 1, sk next ch-1 sp, dc in next sc; rep from * to last ch-1 sp; ch 1, sk last ch-1 sp, in last sc work (dc, ch 1, dc), turn. *(53 [53, 53, 57, 57, 61, 65, 65] sts)*

Rows 7 & 8: Rep rows 5 and 6. *(57 [57, 57, 61, 61, 65, 69, 69] sts at end of row 8)*

Row 9: Rep row 5.

Row 10: Rep row 2.

Row 11: Rep row 3.

Row 12: Rep row 6. *(61 [61, 61, 65, 65, 69, 73, 73] sts at end of row 12)*

Rows 13–28: [Work rows 9–12] 4 times. *(77 [77, 77, 81, 81, 85, 89, 89] sts at end of row 28)*

Row 29: Ch 1, sc in first dc; *ch 1, sk next ch-1 sp, sc in next dc; rep from * to last ch-1 sp; ch 1, sk last ch-1 sp, sc in 3rd ch of turning ch-3, turn.

Row 30: Ch 3, *ch 1, sk next ch-1 sp, dc in next sc; rep from * across, turn.

Rep rows 29 and 30 until piece measures 15 inches from beg.

Fasten off and weave in ends.

Assembly
Sew shoulder seams.

Neck Edging
Row 1: Hold piece with RS facing you; join yarn in first row of Right Front Neck Edging; ch 1, work 23 [23, 24, 24, 25, 26, 27, 28] around Right Front neck edge, work 13 [14, 14, 15, 16, 17, 18, 19] sc across Back neck edge; place marker; work 13 [13, 14, 15, 16, 17, 18, 19] sc across rem Back neck edge; work 23 [23, 24, 24, 25, 26, 27, 28] around Left Front neck edge to row 1 of Neck Shaping, turn. *(72 [74, 76, 78, 82, 86, 90, 94] sc)*

Row 2: Ch 2 *(counts as a sc and a ch-1 sp on this and following rows)*, sk next sc; *ch 1, sk next sc, sc in next sc; rep from * to next marker, ending with sc in sc before marker; ch 1, sc in st after marker; **ch 1, sk next sc, sc in next sc; rep from ** across, turn. *(73 [81, 89, 97, 105, 113, 121, 129] sts)*

Note: *Move marker on each following row.*

Row 3: Ch 2, sk next sc; *ch 1, sk next sc, sc in next sc; rep from * across, turn.

Rows 4 & 5: Rep row 3.

Hood
Row 1: Ch 3 *(counts as a dc on this and following rows)*, *ch 1, sk next ch-1 sp, dc in next sc; rep from * across, turn.

Row 2: Ch 1, sc first dc; *ch 1, sk next ch-1 sp, sc in next dc; rep from * to st before marker; sc in st before marker and in st after marker; continue in pattern across row.

Row 3: Ch 3, *ch 1, sk next ch-1 sp, dc in next sc; rep from * across, turn.

Row 4: Ch 1, sc first dc; *ch 1, sk next ch-1 sp, sc in next dc; rep from * to last ch-1 sp; ch 1, sk last ch-1 sp, sc in 3rd ch of turning ch-3, turn.

Row 5: Rep row 3.

[Work rows 2–5] 7 [6, 5, 4, 3, 2, 1, 0] times.

Rep rows 2 and 3 until Hood measures 13 [13¼, 13¼, 13½, 13½, 14, 14, 14] inches.

Fasten off and weave in ends.

Matching center of Sleeves to shoulder seams, sew in Sleeves. Sew side and Sleeve seams. Folding Hood in half vertically, sew seam across top.

Border
Rnd 1 (RS): Hold piece with RS facing you; join yarn in 1 side seam; ch 1, sc in same sp; ch 1, sk next st; work [sc in next st, ch 1, sk next st] evenly around outer edge and work (sc, ch 1, sc) in each corner; join with sl st in first sc.

Rnd 2: Ch 1, sc in same sc as joining; *ch 1, sc in next sc; rep from * to next corner ch-1 sp; in corner ch-1 sp work (sc, ch 1, sc); **ch 1, sc in next sc; rep from ** to next corner ch-1 sp; in corner ch-1 sp work (sc, ch 1, sc); ***ch 1, sc in next sc; rep from *** to first sc; join with sl st in first sc.

Rnds 3–6: Rep rnd 2.

Fasten off and weave in ends.

Finishing
Referring to photo for placement, sew buttons evenly spaced on Left Front Border. Button through any ch-1 sp on Right Front Border.

GRANNY SQUARES

Chapter 4

SQUARE-DEAL SHRUG

Design by Joyce Nordstrom

Skill Level

EASY

Finished Sizes

Instructions given fit woman's small/medium with size I hook; for large/X-large use size J hook. Information for larger size is in [ ].

Finished Garment Measurements

Chest: 40 inches *(small/medium)* [43 inches *(large/X-large)*]

Materials

• Red Heart Super Saver medium (worsted) weight yarn (7 oz/364 yds/198g per skein):
    1 skein #380 Windsor blue *(A)*
    1 skein #313 Aran *(B)*
    1 skein #657 dusty teal *(C)*
    1 skein #330 linen *(D)*
    1 skein #305 aspen print *(E)*
• Size I/9/5.5mm crochet hook or size needed to obtain gauge (for size small/medium)
• Size J/10/6mm crochet hook or size needed to obtain gauge (for size large/X-large)
• Tapestry needle
• 2 matching ⅞-inch buttons
• Sewing needle and matching thread

Gauge

Size I hook: rnds 1–5 = 6¾ inches
Size J hook: rnds 1–5 = 7¼ inches

Special Stitches

Beginning cluster (beg cl): Ch 2, keeping last lp of each dc on hook, 2 dc in sp indicated; yo and draw through all 3 lps on hook.

Cluster (cl): Keeping last lp of each dc on hook, 3 dc in sp indicated; yo and draw through all 4 lps on hook.

INSTRUCTIONS

Large Motif (Back)

Rnd 1 (RS): With A, ch 5; join with sl st to form ring; ch 4 *(counts as a dc and a ch-1 sp)*, [dc in ring, ch 1] 11 times; join with sl st in 3rd ch of beg ch-4. *(12 dc)*

Rnd 2: Sl st in next ch-1 sp; **beg cl** *(see Special Stitches)* in same sp; ch 3; [**cl** *(see Special Stitches)* in next ch-1 sp, ch 3] 11 times; join in top of beg cl. *(12 cls)*

Fasten off.

Rnd 3: Join B with sl st in in any ch-3 sp; ch 1, sc in same sp; ch 5; [sc in next ch-3 sp, ch 5] 11 times; join with sl st in first sc. Fasten off.

Rnd 4: Join C with sl st in any ch-5 sp; ch 4 *(counts as tr)*, in same sp work (3 tr, ch 3, 4 tr)—*beg corner made*; sc in next ch-5 sp, ch 5, sc in next ch-5 sp; *in next ch-5 sp work (4 tr, ch 3, 4 tr)—*corner made*; sc in next ch-5 sp, ch 5, sc in next ch-5 sp; rep from * twice; join with sl st in 4th ch of beg ch-4. Fasten off.

Rnd 5: Join B with sl st in any corner ch-3 sp; ch 3 *(counts as a dc on this and following rnds)*; in same sp work (2 dc, ch 3, 3 dc)—*dc corner made*; *ch 1, sk next 2 tr, 3 dc in next tr, ch 1, sk next tr, 3 dc in next ch-5 sp; ch 1, sk next sc and next tr; 3 dc in next tr; sk next 2 tr, in next corner ch-3 sp work (3 dc, ch 3, 3 dc)—*dc corner made*; rep from * twice; ch 1, sk next 2 tr, 3 dc in next tr, ch 1, sk next tr, 3 dc in

next ch-5 sp; ch 1, sk next sc and next tr; 3 dc in next tr; sk next 2 tr; join with sl st in 3rd dc of beg ch-3.

Rnd 6: Sl st in next 2 dc and in next ch-3 sp; dc corner in same sp; *[ch 1, 3 dc in next ch-1 sp] 4 times; ch 1, in next corner ch-3 sp work dc corner; rep from * twice; [ch 1, 3 dc in next ch-1 sp] 4 times; ch 1; join with sl st in 3rd ch of beg ch-3. Fasten off.

Rnd 7: Join D with sl st in any corner ch-3 sp; dc corner in same sp; *[ch 1, 3 dc in next ch-1 sp] 5 times; ch 1, in next corner ch-3 sp work dc corner; rep from * twice; [ch 1, 3 dc in next ch-1 sp] 5 times; ch 1; join with sl st in 3rd ch of beg ch-3.

Rnd 8: Sl st in next 2 dc and in next ch-3 sp; dc corner in same sp; *[ch 1, 3 dc in next ch-1 sp] 6 times; ch 1, in next corner ch-3 sp work dc corner; rep from * twice; [ch 1, 3 dc in next ch-1 sp] 6 times; ch 1; join with sl st in 3rd ch of beg ch-3. Fasten off.

Rnd 9: Join A with sl st in any corner ch-3 sp; dc corner in same sp; *[ch 1, 3 dc in next ch-1 sp] 7 times; ch 1, in next corner ch-3 sp work dc corner; rep from * twice; [ch 1, 3 dc in next ch-1 sp] 7 times; ch 1; join with sl st in 3rd ch of beg ch-3.

Rnd 10: Sl st in next 2 dc and in next ch-3 sp; dc corner in same sp; *[ch 1, 3 dc in next ch-1 sp] 8 times; ch 1, in next corner ch-3 sp work dc corner; rep from * twice; [ch 1, 3 dc in next ch-1 sp] 8 times; ch 1; join with sl st in 3rd ch of beg ch-3. Fasten off.

Note: Remainder of Large Motif is worked in rows.

Row 1: Join E with sl st in any corner ch-3 sp; ch 3, 2 dc in same corner; *ch 1; [3 dc in next ch-1 sp, ch 1] 9 times; in next corner ch-3 sp work dc corner; rep from * once; ch 1, [3 dc in next ch-1 sp, ch 1]

American School of Needlework, Berne, IN 46711 • ASNpub.com

9 times; 3 dc in next corner ch-3 sp, turn, leaving rem side unworked.

Row 2: Ch 3; *[3 dc in next ch-1 sp, ch 1] 10 times; in next corner ch-3 sp work dc corner; ch 1; rep from * once; ch 1, [3 dc in next ch-1 sp, ch 1] 10 times; dc in 3rd ch of beg ch-3.

Fasten off and weave in all ends.

Small Motif
Make 2.

Work same as Large Motif through rnd 5. At end of rnd 5, fasten off and weave in all ends.

Left Front

Upper Section

Row 1 (RS): Hold 1 Small Motif with RS facing you; join B with sl st in any corner ch-3 sp; ch 3, 2 dc in same sp; [ch 1, 3 dc in next ch-1 sp] 4 times; ch 1, 3 dc in next corner ch-3 sp. Fasten off, leaving rem sides unworked.

Row 2: Hold piece with RS facing you; join D with sl st in sp formed by beg ch-3 of row 1; ch 4, [3 dc in next ch-1 sp, ch 1] 5 times; sk next 2 dc, dc in last dc, turn.

Row 3: Ch 4, [3 dc in next ch-1 sp, ch 1] 5 times; 3 dc in sp formed by beg ch-4. Fasten off.

Row 4: Hold piece with RS facing you; join A with sl st in first dc; ch 4, [3 dc in next ch-1 sp, ch 1] 5 times; sk next 2 dc, dc in last dc, turn.

Row 5: Ch 3, 2 dc in next ch-1 sp; [ch 1, 3 dc in next ch-1 sp] 4 times; ch 1, 3 dc in sp formed by beg ch-4. Fasten off.

Neck Shaping

Row 1 (RS): Hold piece with RS facing you; join E with sl st in first dc; ch 4, [3 dc in next ch-1 sp, ch 1] 3 times; dc in next ch-1 sp, turn, leaving rem sps unworked.

Row 2: Ch 3, [3 dc in next ch-1 sp, ch 1] twice; 3 dc in sp formed by beg ch-4.

Fasten off and weave in all ends.

Lower Section

Row 1 (RS): Hold Motif with RS facing you and unworked side opposite worked side at top; join B with sl st in any corner ch-3 sp; ch 3, 2 dc in same sp; [ch 1, 3 dc in next ch-1 sp] 4 times; ch 1, 3 dc in next corner ch-3 sp. Fasten off, leaving rem sides unworked.

Rows 2–5: Rep rows 2–5 of Upper Section.

Right Front

Work same as Left Front to Neck Shaping.

Neck Shaping

Row 1 (RS): Hold piece with RS facing you; join E with sl st in 2nd ch-1 sp on row 5; ch 4, [3 dc in next ch-1 sp, ch 1] 3 times; dc in last dc, turn.

Row 2: Sl st in next ch-1 sp, ch 3, 2 dc in same sp; ch 1, [3 dc in next ch-1 sp, ch 1] twice; dc in sp formed by beg ch-4.

Fasten off and weave in all ends.

Lower Section

Work same as Lower Section of Left Front.

Sleeve
Make 2.

Rnds 1–5: Rep rnds 1–5 of Large Motif. At end of rnd 5, fasten off.

First Section

Note: *Remainder of piece is worked in rows.*

Row 1 (RS): Hold piece with RS facing you; join B with sl st in any corner ch-3 sp; ch 3, 2 dc in same sp; [ch 1, 3 dc in next ch-1 sp] 5 times. Fasten off.

Row 2: Hold piece with RS facing you; join E with sl st in 3rd ch of beg ch-3; ch 4, [3 dc in next ch-1 sp, ch 1] 4 times; sk next 2 dc, dc in last dc, turn.

Row 3: Ch 3, 2 dc in next ch-1 sp; [ch 1, 3 dc in next ch-1 sp] 4 times; ch 1, 3 dc in sp formed by beg ch-4. Fasten off.

Row 4: Hold piece with RS facing you; join A with sl st in first dc; ch 4, [3 dc in next ch-1 sp, ch 1] 5 times; sk next 2 dc, dc in 3rd ch of turning ch-3, turn.

Row 5: Ch 3, 3 dc in next ch-1 sp; [ch 1, 3 dc in next ch-1 sp] 4 times; ch 1, 3 dc in sp formed by beg ch-4. Fasten off.

Row 6: Hold piece with RS facing you; join E with sl st in first dc; ch 4, [3 dc in next sp formed by turning ch, ch 1] 5 times; sk next 3 dc, dc in 3rd ch of turning ch-3, turn.

Row 7: Ch 3, 2 dc in next ch-1 sp; [ch 1, 3 dc in next ch-1 sp] 4 times; ch 1, 3 dc in sp formed by beg ch-4, turn.

Row 8: Ch 4, [3 dc in next ch-1 sp, ch 1] 5 times; sk next 2 dc, dc in 3rd ch of turning ch-3, turn.

Row 9: Ch 3, 2 dc in next ch-1 sp; [ch 1, 3 dc in next ch-1 sp] 4 times; ch 1, 3 dc in sp formed by beg ch-4, turn.

Row 10: Ch 4, [3 dc in next ch-1 sp, ch 1] 5 times; sk next 2 dc, dc in 3rd ch of turning ch-3.

Fasten off.

2nd Section

Row 1 (RS): Hold piece with RS facing you and unworked side opposite worked side at top; join B with sl st in any corner ch-3 sp; ch 3, 2 dc in same sp; [ch 1, 3 dc in next ch-1 sp] 5 times. Fasten off.

Rows 2–10: Rep rows 2–10 of First Section.

Side Edging

Hold 1 Sleeve with RS facing you and row 10 of First Section to right; join E with sl st in sp formed by turning ch-4 of row 10; ch 3, 2 dc in same sp; [ch 1, 3 dc in next ch-1 sp] 16 times. Fasten off.

Hold rem Sleeve with RS facing you and row 10 to left; join E with sl st in sp formed by turning ch-4 of row 10; ch 3, 2 dc in same sp; [ch 1, 3 dc in next ch-1 sp] 16 times.

Fasten off and weave in all ends.

Sew shoulder seams.

Left Side & Underarm Sections

Row 1 (RS): Hold piece with RS of Left Front facing you and shoulder seam to left; join E with sl st in sp formed by turning ch of last row to right; ch 4, [3 dc in sp, ch 1] 22 times; 3 dc in next corner ch-3 sp, turn.

Row 2: Ch 4, [3 dc in next ch-1 sp, ch 1] 22 times; 3 dc in sp formed by beg ch-4, turn.

Row 3: Ch 4, [3 dc in next ch-1 sp, ch 1] 3 times; dc in next ch-1 sp; turn.

Row 4: Ch 3, [3 dc in next ch-1 sp, ch 1] 3 times; 3 dc in next ch-1 sp, turn.

Row 5: Ch 4, [3 dc in next ch-1 sp, ch 1] 3 times; sk next 3 dc, dc in 3rd ch of turning ch-3. Fasten off.

Underarm Section

Row 1: Hold piece with RS of Back facing you and shoulder seam to right; sk first 3 3-dc groups from left edge; join E with sl st in next ch-1 sp to left; ch 3, 2 dc in same sp; ch 1, [3 dc in next ch-1 sp, ch 1] twice; 3 dc in sp formed by turning ch-4; turn.

Row 2: Ch 4, [3 dc in next ch-1 sp, ch 1] 3 times; sk next 2 dc, dc in 3rd ch of beg ch-3, turn.

Row 3: Ch 3, 2 dc in next ch-1 sp; ch 1, [3 dc in next ch-1 sp, ch 1] twice; 3 dc in sp formed by turning ch-4. Fasten off.

Right Side & Underarm Sections

Row 1 (RS): Hold piece with RS of Back facing you and shoulder seam to left; join E with sl st in first ch-1 sp of last row to right; ch 3, 2 dc in same sp; ch 1, [3 dc in sp, ch 1] 22 times; dc in last dc of last row of Right Front, turn.

Row 2: Ch 3, 2 dc in next ch-1 sp; ch 1, [3 dc in next ch-1 sp, ch 1] 23 times; ch 1, dc in 3rd of beg ch-3, turn.

Row 3: Sl st in next ch-1 sp, ch 3, 2 dc in same sp; ch 1, [3 dc in next ch-1 sp, ch 1] twice; 3 dc in next ch-1 sp; turn.

Row 4: Ch 4, [3 dc in next ch-1 sp, ch 1] 3 times; dc in 3rd ch of beg ch-3, turn.

Row 5: Ch 3, 2 dc in next ch-1 sp; ch 1, [3 dc in next ch-1 sp, ch 1] twice; 3 dc in sp formed by turning ch-4. Fasten off.

Underarm Section

Row 1: Hold piece with RS of Right Front facing you and shoulder seam to right; sk first three 3-dc groups from left edge; join E with sl st in next ch-1 sp to left; ch 3, 2 dc in same sp; ch 1, [3 dc in next ch-1 sp, ch 1] twice; 3 dc in sp formed by turning ch-4; turn.

Row 2: Ch 4, [3 dc in next ch-1 sp, ch 1] 3 times; sk next 2 dc, dc in 3rd ch of beg ch-3, turn.

Row 3: Ch 3, 2 dc in next ch-1 sp; ch 1, [3 dc in next ch-1 sp, ch 1] twice; 3 dc in sp formed by turning ch-4. Fasten off.

Assembly

With tapestry needle and E, sew side seams. Matching center of Sleeves to shoulder seams, sew Sleeves in place, forming square armholes.

Borders

Body Border

Rnd 1: Hold piece with RS facing you and lower edge at top; join E with sl st in first sp to left of right underarm seam;

ch 3, 2 dc in same sp; ch 1, *3 dc in next sp; ch 1; rep from * to next corner sp; in corner sp work (3 dc, ch 1, 3 dc)—*corner made*; ch 1; working up Right Front edge, in each sp to next corner work (3 dc, ch 1); in corner work (3 dc, ch 1, 3 dc)—*corner made*; ch 1; working around neck edge to next corner, in each sp work (3 dc, ch 1); in corner work (3 dc, ch 1, 3 dc)—*corner made*; ch 1; working down Left Front edge, in each sp to next corner work (3 dc, ch 1); in corner work (3 dc, ch 1, 3 dc)—*corner made*; ch 1; working across lower edge, in each sp to beg ch-3 work (3 dc, ch 1); join with sl st in 3rd ch of beg ch-3.

Rnd 2: Sl st in next 2 dc and in next ch-1 sp; ch 3, 2 dc in same sp; ch 1, in each ch-1 sp work (3 dc, ch 1) and in each corner ch-1 sp work [3 dc, ch 1] twice; join with sl st in 3rd ch of beg ch-3. Change to C by drawing lp through; cut E.

Rnd 3: Working in **front lps** *(see page 28)* only, sl st in each dc and in each ch; join in joining sl st.

Fasten off and weave in ends.

Sleeve Border

Rnd 1 (RS): Hold 1 Sleeve with RS facing you; join E with sl st in first sp to right of underarm seam; ch 3, 2 dc in same sp; ch 1; in each rem sp work (3 dc, ch 1); join in 3rd ch of beg ch-3. Change to C by drawing lp through; cut E.

Rnd 2: Working in front lps only, sl st in each dc and in each ch; join in joining sl st.

Fasten off and weave in ends.

Rep on rem Sleeve.

Finishing

With sewing needle and matching thread and referring to photo for placement, sew buttons to Left Front.

JOIN-AS-YOU-GO SCARF

Design by Mary Ann Frits

Skill Level

EASY

Finished Size

Approximately 4 x 72 inches

Materials

- Patons Grace light (light worsted) weight cotton yarn (1¾ oz/136 yds/50g per skein):
  2 skeins #60901 tangelo *(A)*
  1 skein #60008 natural *(B)*
- Size F/5/3.75 crochet hook or size needed to obtain gauge
- Tapestry needle

Gauge

Motif = 3 inches

INSTRUCTIONS

Motif A

Rnd 1: With A, ch 8; join to form ring; ch 1, sc in same ch as joining, ch 9, [sc in ring, ch 9] 7 times; join in first sc.

Rnd 2: Sl st in next 4 chs of next ch-9 sp, ch 1, sc in same sp; ch 5, [sc in 5th ch of next ch-9 sp, ch 5] 7 times; join in first sc.

Rnd 3: Sl st in next ch-5 sp, ch 1, in same sp work (sc, ch 5, sc); *ch 5, sc in next ch-5 sp, ch 5, in next ch-5 sp work (sc, ch 5, sc); rep from * twice; ch 5, sc in next ch-5 sp, ch 5; join in first sc.

Rnd 4: Sl st in next ch-5 sp, ch 1, in same sp work (sc, ch 5, sc); *[ch 5, sc in next ch-5 sp] twice; ch 5, in next ch-5 sp work (sc, ch 5, sc); rep from * twice; [ch 5, sc in next ch-5 sp] twice; ch 5; join in first sc.

Rnd 5: Sl st in next ch-5 sp, ch 1, in same sp work (sc, ch 7, sc)—*corner made*; *[ch 5, sc in next ch-5 sp] 3 times; ch 5, in next ch-5 sp work (sc, ch 7, sc)—*corner made*; rep from * twice; [ch 5, sc in next ch-5 sp] 3 times; ch 5; join in first sc.

Fasten off and weave in ends.

Motif B

Work same as Motif A through rnd 4.

Rnd 5: Sl st in next ch-5 sp, ch 1, in same sp work (sc, ch 7, sc)—*corner made*; [ch 5, sc in next ch-5 sp] 3 times; ch 5, in next ch-5 sp work (sc, ch 7, sc)—*corner made*; [ch 5, sc in next ch-5 sp] 3 times; ch 5, sc in next ch-5 sp, ch 3; hold WS of Motif A facing WS of working motif, carefully matching sts; sl st in corresponding corner ch-7 sp on Motif A, ch 3; on working motif, sc in same ch-5 sp; [ch 2; on Motif A, sl st in next ch-5 sp, ch 2; on working motif, sc in next ch-5 sp] 3 times; ch 2; on Motif A, sl st in next ch-5 sp, ch 3; on working motif, sc in next ch-5 sp, ch 3; on Motif A, sl st in next corner ch-7 sp, ch 3; on working motif, sc in same ch-5 sp, [ch 5, sc in next ch-5 sp] 3 times; ch 5; join in first sc.

Fasten off and weave in ends.

Motif C

Work same as Motif A through rnd 4.

Rnd 5: Sl st in next ch-5 sp, ch 1, in same sp work (sc, ch 7, sc)—*corner made*; [ch 5, sc in next ch-5 sp] 3 times; ch 5, in next ch-5 sp work (sc, ch 7, sc)—*corner made*; [ch 5, sc in next ch-5 sp] 3 times; ch 5, sc in next ch-5 sp, ch 3; hold WS of Motif B facing WS of working motif, carefully matching sts on side opposite joined side; sl st in corresponding corner ch-7 sp on Motif A, ch 3; on working motif, sc in same ch-5 sp; [ch 2; on Motif A, sl st in next ch-5 sp, ch 2; on working motif, sc in next ch-5 sp] 3 times; ch 2; on Motif A, sl st in next ch-5 sp, ch 2; on working motif, sc in next ch-5 sp, ch 3; on Motif A, sl st in next corner ch-7 sp, ch 3; on working motif, sc in same ch-5 sp, [ch 5, sc in next ch-5 sp] 3 times; ch 5; join in first sc.

Fasten off and weave in ends.

Work rem 13 motifs same as Motif C.

Edging

Rnd 1: Hold piece with RS facing you and 1 short end at top; join B in ch-7 sp in upper right-hand corner; ch 1, 4 sc in same sp; [hdc in next sc, 3 sc in next ch-5 sp] 4 times; hdc in next sc, 4 sc in next corner ch-7 sp; working around rem sides, work hdc in each sc and in each sl st joining, 2 sc in each joined corner sp, 3 sc in each ch-5 sp and 4 sc in each rem corner ch-7 sps; join in first sc.

Rnd 2: Ch 5 *(counts as a tr and a ch-1 sp)*, in same sp work [tr, ch 1] 3 times; tr in same sc; sk next 3 sc, sl st in next sc, sk next 3 sc; *in next sc work [tr, ch 1] 4 times; tr in same sc; sk next 3 sc, sl st in next sc; rep from * around; join in 4th ch of beg ch-5.

Fasten off and weave in ends.

FANTASY AFGHAN

Design by Svetlana Avrakh

Skill Level

EASY

Finished Size

Approximately 46 x 63 inches

Materials

- Patons Decor medium (worsted) weight yarn (3½ oz/210 yds/100g per skein): **[4 MEDIUM]**
  5 balls #01645 pale country pink *(A)*
  5 balls #01646 country pink *(B)*
- Patons Divine bulky (chunky) weight yarn (3½ oz/142 yds/100g per skein): **[5 BULKY]**
  4 balls #06740 floral fantasy *(C)*
- Size I/9/5.5mm crochet hook or size needed to obtain gauge
- Tapestry needle

Gauge

13 dc = 4 inches

Special Stitches

Beginning cluster (beg cl):

Ch 5, keeping last lp of each dtr on hook, 2 dtr in ring; yo and draw through all 3 lps on hook.

Cluster (cl):

Keeping last lp of each dtr on hook, 3 dtr in ring; yo and draw through all 4 lps on hook.

Patten Note

To change color, work last stitch until 2 loops remain on hook; with new color, yarn over and draw through 2 loops on hook. Carry unused yarns loosely up side until needed again.

INSTRUCTIONS

Motif A
Make 15.

Rnd 1 (RS): With B, ch 6; join with sl st to form ring; ch 3 *(counts as a dc on this and following rnds)*, 15 dc in ring, changing to A in last dc; join with sl st in 3rd ch of beg ch-3. *(16 dc)*

Fasten off B.

Rnd 2: Ch 4 *(counts as a dc and a ch-1 sp)*, [dc in next dc, ch 1] 15 times; join with sl st in 3rd ch of ch 4. Fasten off.

Rnd 3: Join C with sl st in any ch-1 sp; ch 3, dc in same sp; 2 dc in next rem ch-1 sp; join with sl st in 3rd ch of beg ch-3. *(32 dc)*

Rnd 4: Ch 1, sc in same ch; *ch 5, sl st in top of last sc; ch 4, sk next 2 dc, sc in next dc, ch 3, sc in next dc, ch 4, sk next 2 dc, sc in next dc; rep from * twice; ch 5, sl st in top of last sc; ch 4, sk next 2 dc, sc in next dc, ch 3, sc in next dc, ch 4, sk next 2 dc; join with sl st in first sc.

Rnd 5: Sl st in next ch-5 sp, ch 3, in same sp work (4 dc, ch 3, 5 dc)—*corner made*; *sc in next ch-4 sp, 5 dc in next ch-3 sp; sc in next ch-4 sp, in next ch-5 sp work (5 dc, ch 3, 5 dc)—*corner made*; rep from * twice; sc in next ch-4 sp, 5 dc in next ch-3 sp; sc in next ch-4 sp; join with sl st in 3rd ch of beg ch-3. Fasten off.

Rnd 6: Join A with sl st in ch-3 sp of any corner; ch 1, in same sp work (sc, ch 3, sc)—*sc corner made*; *ch 6, dc in next sc, ch 3, sk next 2 dc, sc in next dc, ch 3, dc in next sc, ch 6, in next ch-3 sp work (sc, ch 3, sc)—*sc corner made*; rep from * twice; ch 6, dc in next sc, ch 3, sk next 2 dc, sc in next dc, ch 3, dc in next sc, ch 6; join with sl st in first sc.

Rnd 7: Sl st in next ch-3 sp, ch 3, in same sp work (dc, ch 3, 2 dc)—*beg dc corner made*; *6 dc in next ch-6 sp; 4 dc in each of next 2 ch-3 sps; 6 dc in next ch-6 sp; in next ch-3 sp work (2 dc, ch 3, 2 dc)—*dc corner made*; rep from * twice; 6 dc in next ch-6 sp; 4 dc in each of next 2 ch-3 sps; 6 dc in next ch-6 sp; join with sl st in 3rd ch of beg ch-3. Fasten off.

Rnd 8: Join B with sl st in any corner ch-3 sp; ch 2 *(counts as an hdc)*, in same sp work (hdc, ch 3, 2 hdc)—*beg hdc corner made*; *hdc in each dc to next corner ch-3 sp, in corner ch-3 sp work (2 hdc, ch 3; 2 hdc)—*hdc corner made*; rep from * twice; hdc in each dc to beg ch-2; join with sl st in 2nd ch of beg ch-2.

Fasten off and weave in all ends.

Motif B
Make 15.

Rnd 1: With C, ch 5; join to form a ring; **beg cl** (see Special Stitches) in ring; ch 3, [**cl** (see Special Stitches) in ring, ch 3] 7 times; join in top of beg ch. (8 cls)

Fasten off.

Rnd 2: Join A with sl st in any ch-3 sp; ch 3 (counts as a dc on this and following rnds), 3 dc in same ch-3 sp; 4 dc in next ch-3 sp; ch 5; *4 dc in each of next 2 ch-3 sps, ch 5; rep from * around; join with sl st in 3rd ch of beg ch-3. Fasten off.

Rnd 3: Join B with sl st in any ch-5 sp; ch 3, in same sp work (2 dc, ch 3, 3 dc)—beg corner made; dc in next 8 dc, in next ch-5 sp work (3 dc, ch 3, 3 dc)—corner made; rep from * twice; dc in next 8 dc; join with sl st in 3rd ch of beg ch-3. Fasten off.

Rnd 4: Join A with sl st in any corner ch-3 sp; ch 3, ch 3, dc in same sp; *dc in each dc to next corner ch-3 sp; in corner ch-3 sp work (dc, ch 3, dc); rep from * twice; dc in each dc to beg ch-3; join with sl st in 3rd ch of beg ch-3. Fasten off.

Rnd 5: With B, rep rnd 4.

Rnd 6: With A, rep rnd 4.

Rnd 7: With B, rep rnd 4.

Rnd 8: Join A with sl st in any corner ch-3 sp; ch 3, in same sp work (dc, ch 3, 2 dc); *dc in each dc to next corner ch-3 sp; in corner ch-3 sp work (2 dc, ch 3, 2 dc); rep from * twice; dc in each dc to beg ch-3; join with sl st in 3rd ch of beg ch-3.

Fasten off and weave in all ends.

Assembly
Referring to assembly diagram for placement, join Motifs in 6 rows of 5 motifs each. To join Motifs, hold 1 Motif A and 1 Motif B with WS tog, carefully matching sts. Working through both thickness at same time, join B in right-hand corner ch-3 sp; ch 1, sc in same sp, in each st across side and in next corner ch-3 sp. Fasten off. Join rem Motifs in same manner, making sure all 4-corner joinings are secure.

Border
Rnd 1 (RS): Hold piece with RS facing you and 1 short end at top; join B with sl st in upper right-hand corner ch-3 sp; ch 1, in same sp work (sc, ch 3, sc)—corner made; *hdc in each st and in each joined corner ch-3 sp to next outer corner ch-3 sp; in outer corner ch-3 sp work (sc, ch 3, sc)—corner made; rep from * twice; hdc in each st and in each joined corner ch-3 sp to first sc; join with sl st in first sc. Fasten off.

Rnd 2: Join C with sl st in any corner ch-3 sp, ch 4 (counts as a dc and a ch-1 sp), dc in same sp?—beg dc corner made; *ch 1, sk next hdc, dc in next hdc; rep from * to next corner ch-3 sp; in corner ch-3 sp work (dc, ch 3, dc)—dc corner made; **ch 1, sk next hdc, dc in next hdc; rep from ** to next corner ch-3 sp; in corner ch-3 sp work (dc, ch 3, dc)—dc corner made; ***ch 1, sk next hdc, dc in next hdc; rep from *** to next corner ch-3 sp; in corner

ch-3 sp work (dc, ch 3, dc)—dc corner made; ****ch 1, sk next hdc, dc in next hdc; rep from **** to beg ch-4; join with sl st in 3rd ch of ch-4. Fasten off.

Rnd 3: Join A with sl st in any sk hdc on rnd 1; ch 1, sc in same st; *ch 1, sk next dc pushing **post** (see page 28) of dc to RS, sc in next sk hdc on rnd 1; rep from * to next corner ch-3 sp; working over corner ch-3 sp on rnd 2, in corner ch-3 sp on rnd 1 work (sc, ch 3, sc)—sc corner made; **ch 1, sk next dc pushing post of dc to RS, sc in next sk hdc on rnd 1; rep from ** to next corner ch-3 sp; working over corner ch-3 sp on rnd 2, in corner ch-3 sp on rnd 1 work (sc, ch 3, sc)—sc corner made; ***ch 1, sk next dc pushing post of dc to RS, sc in next sk hdc on rnd 1; rep from *** to next corner ch-3 sp; working over corner ch-3 sp on rnd 2, in corner ch-3 sp on rnd 1 work (sc, ch 3, sc)—sc corner made; ****ch 1, sk next dc pushing post of dc to RS, sc in next sk hdc on rnd 1; rep from **** to first sc; join with sl st in first sc. Fasten off.

Rnd 4: Join B with sl st in any corner ch-3 sp; ch 2 (counts as a hdc), hdc in each hdc and in each ch-1 sp; work (hdc, ch 3, hdc) in each corner ch-3 sp; join with sl st in 2nd ch of beg ch-2.

Fasten off and weave in all ends.

B	A	B	A	B
A	B	A	B	A
B	A	B	A	B
A	B	A	B	A
B	A	B	A	B
A	B	A	B	A

Fantasy Afghan
Assembly Diagram

JAZZY DIAMONDS

Design by Mary Ann Frits

Skill Level

EASY

Finished Sizes

Instructions given fit woman's small; changes for medium and large are in [ ]. Size is determined by hook size used.

Finished Garment Measurements

Chest: 36 *(small)* [40 *(medium)*, 44 *(large)*] inches

Materials

- Red Heart LusterSheen fine (sport) weight yarn (4 oz/335 yds/113g per skein): 3 [3, 4] skeins #0007 vanilla
- Size D/3/3.25mm [E/4/3.5mm, F/5/3.75mm] crochet hook or size needed to obtain gauge
- Tapestry needle

Gauge

Size D hook: Motif = 3 inches
Size E hook: Motif = 3½ inches
Size F hook: Motif = 4 inches

Pattern Note

Refer to individual diagrams for placement and number of Motifs required for each section of garment.

INSTRUCTIONS

Back

Motif A

Row 1 (RS): Ch 14; dc in 6th ch from hook *(beg 5 sk chs count as a ch-1 sp, a dc and a ch-1 sp)*, [ch 1, sk next ch, dc in next ch] 4 times, turn.

Row 2: Ch 4 *(counts as a dc and a ch-1 sp on this and following rows)*, [dc in next dc, ch 1] 4 times; sk next ch of beg 5 sk chs, dc in next ch, turn.

Row 3: Ch 4, [dc in next dc, ch 1] 4 times; dc in 3rd ch of turning ch-4, turn.

Row 4: Rep row 3.

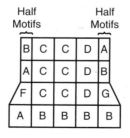

Right Front   **Left Front**

Sleeve

Back

Row 5: Ch 4, [dc in next dc, ch 1] 4 times; dc in 3rd ch of turning ch-4. Do not turn.

Note: Remainder of Motif is worked in rnds.

Rnd 1: Ch 1, working around edge of piece, 2 sc in each of next 4 sps; *5 sc in next sp—corner made*; 2 sc in each of next 3 sps; rep from * twice; 3 sc in same sp as beg 2 sc made—*corner made*; join with sl st in first sc.

Rnd 2: Ch 1, sl st in next 3 sc; *ch 6, sk next 2 sc, sl st in next 4 sc, ch 1, sc in next sc, ch 1, sl st in next 4 sc; rep from * twice; ch 6, sk next 2 sc, sl st in next 4 sc, ch 1, sc in next sc, ch 1; sl st in next sc; join with sl st in joining sl st.

Rnd 3: Sl st in next 2 sts and in next 2 chs of next ch-6 sp; ch 7; *sk next 2 chs, sc in next ch, ch 6, sk next ch, next 4 sl sts and next ch, sc in next sc, ch 6, sk next ch, next 4 sl sts, and first ch of next ch-6 sp, sc in next ch, ch 6; rep from * twice; sk next 2 chs, sc in next ch, ch 6, sk next ch, next 4 sl sts and next ch, sc in next sc, ch 6; join with sl st in first ch of beg ch-7.

Rnd 4: Sl st in next sp; ch 1, in same sp work (3 sc, ch 3, 3 sc)—*corner made*; *7 sc in each of next 2 ch-6 sps; in next ch-6 sp work (3 sc, ch 3, 3 sc)—*corner made*; rep from * twice; 7 sc in each of next 2 ch-6 sps; join with sl st in first sc. Fasten off.

Motif B

Work same as Motif A through rnd 3.

Rnd 4: Sl st in next sp; ch 1, in same sp work (3 sc, ch 3, 3 sc)—*corner made*; *7 sc in each of next 2 ch-6 sps; 3 sc in next ch-6 sp; ch 1; holding WS of last completed Motif facing WS of working Motif and matching sts, sl st in 2nd ch of corresponding corner ch-3 sp on completed Motif, ch 1; on working Motif, 3 sc in same sp as previous sc worked—*joined corner made*; [4 sc in next ch-6 sp, sc around **post** *(see page 28)* of 4th sc of corresponding ch-6 sp on completed Motif, on working Motif, 3 sc in same sp as previous 3 sc made] twice; 3 sc in next ch-6 sp; ch 1; sl st in 2nd ch of corresponding corner ch-3 sp on completed Motif, ch 1; on working Motif, 3 sc in same sp as previous sc worked—*joined corner made*; 7 sc in each of next 2 ch-6 sps; in next ch-6 sp work (3 sc, ch 3, 3 sc)—*corner made*; 7 sc in each of next 2 ch-6 sps; join with sl st in first sc. Fasten off.

Motif C

Work same as Motif A through rnd 3.

Rnd 4: Sl st in next sp; ch 1, in same sp work (3 sc, ch 3, 3 sc)—*corner made*; 7 sc in each of next 2 ch-6 sp; in next ch-6 sp work (3 sc, ch 3, 3 sc)—*corner made*; 7 sc in each of next 2 ch-6 sps; 3 sc in next ch-6 sp; ch 1; holding WS of completed Motif *(see Back diagram)* facing WS of working Motif and matching sts, sl st in 2nd ch of corresponding corner ch-3 sp on completed Motif, ch 1; on working Motif, 3 sc in same sp as previous sc worked—*joined corner made*; [4 sc in next ch-6 sp, sc around post of 4th sc of corresponding ch-6 sp on completed Motif, on working Motif, 3 sc in same sp as previous 3 sc made] twice; 3 sc in next ch-6 sp; ch 1, sc in center of joining sc of corresponding ch-3 sps on completed Motifs, ch 1, on working Motif, 3 sc in same sp as previous sc made; 7 sc in each of next 2 ch-6 sps; join with sl st in first sc. Fasten off.

Motifs D–E

Referring to Back diagram for number and placement, work same as Motif C, joining sides in same manner.

Right Front

Motifs A–C

Referring to Right Front diagram for number and placement, work same as Motifs A, B and C of Back.

Motif E

Referring to Right Front diagram for number and placement, work same as Motif C, joining sides in same manner.

Half Motif A

Row 1 (RS): Ch 14; dc in 6th ch from hook *(beg 5 sk chs count as a ch-1 sp, a dc and a ch-1 sp)*, [ch 1, sk next ch, dc in next ch] 4 times, turn.

Row 2: Ch 3 *(counts as a dc)*, [dc in next dc, ch 1] 3 times; dc in next dc and in 3rd ch of beg 5 sk chs, turn.

Row 3: Sl st in next dc; ch 3, dc in next dc, ch 1, dc in next dc, sk next dc, dc in 3rd ch of turning ch-3, turn.

Row 4: Sl st in next dc; ch 3, dc in next dc, ch 1, turn, leaving turning ch-3 unworked.

Note: Next part of Motif is worked in rnds. Mark beg of rnds.

Rnd 1: Ch 1, working around edge of piece, 2 sc in each of next 3 sps; 5 sc in next sp—*corner made*; 2 sc in each of next 3 sps; 5 sc in next sp—*corner made*; 2 sc in each of next 2 sps; 3 sc in same sp as beg 2 sc made—*corner made*; join with sl st in first sc.

Rnd 2: Sl st in next 3 sc; ch 6, sk next 2 sc, sl st in next 2 sc, ch 1, sc in next sc—*sc corner made*; ch 1, sl st in next 10 sc, ch 1, sc in next sc—*sc corner made*; ch 1, sl st in next 2 sc, ch 6, sk next 2 sc, sl st in next 4 sc, ch 1, sc in next sc—*sc corner made*; ch 1, sl st in next sc; join with sl st in first sl st. Fasten off.

Note: Remainder of Motif is worked in rows.

Row 1: Hold piece with WS facing you and straight edge at bottom; join yarn with sl st in corner sc of right-hand bottom corner; ch 7, sc in 2nd ch of next ch-6 sp, ch 6, sk next 2 chs, sc in next ch, ch 6, sc in next corner sc, ch 2, sc in 2nd ch of next ch-6 sp, ch 6, sk next 2 chs, sc in next ch, ch 6, sc in next sc corner, turn.

Joining row: 7 sc in next ch-6 sp; 3 sc in next ch-6 sp; ch 1; holding WS of completed Motif *(see Right Front diagram)* facing WS of working Motif and matching sts, sc in 2nd ch of corresponding corner ch-3 sp on completed Motif, ch 1; on working Motif, 3 sc in same sp as previous sc made; [4 sc in next ch-6 sp, sc around post of 4th sc on corresponding ch-6 sp on completed motif; on working Motif, 3 sc in same sp as previous sc made] twice; 3 sc in next ch-6 sp; ch 1, sc in center of joining sc of corresponding ch-3 sps on completed Motifs, ch 1, on working Motif, 3 sc in same sp as previous sc made; 7 sc in next ch-6 sp. Fasten off.

Half Motif B

Work same as Half Motif A to joining row.

Joining row: 4 sc in next ch-6 sp; holding WS of Half Motif A *(see Right Front diagram)* facing WS of working Motif and matching sts, sc around post of 4th sc of corresponding ch-6 sp on Half Motif A, on working Motif, 3 sc in same sp as previous sc made; 3 sc in next ch-6 sp; ch 1, sc in center of joining sc of corresponding ch-3 sps on completed Motifs, ch 1, on working Motif, 3 sc in same sp as previous sc made; [4 sc in next ch-6 sp, sc around post of 4th sc on corresponding ch-6 sp on completed motif, on working Motif, 3 sc in same sp as previous sc made] twice; 3 sc in next ch-6 sp; ch 1, sc in center of joining sc of corresponding ch-3 sps on completed

Motifs, ch 1, on working Motif, 3 sc in same sp as previous sc made; 7 sc in next ch-6 sp. Fasten off.

Left Front

Referring to Left Front diagram for number and placement, work Motifs in same manner as Right Front.

Sleeve
Make 2.

Referring to Sleeve diagram for placement, work Motifs A–D and Half Motifs A and B.

Motif F

Row 1 (RS): Ch 14; dc in 6th ch from hook *(beg 5 sk chs count as a ch-1 sp, a dc and a ch-1 sp)*, [ch 1, sk next ch, dc in next ch] 4 times, turn.

Row 2: Ch 4 *(counts as a dc on this and following rows)*, [dc in next dc, ch 1] 4 times; sk next ch of beg 5 sk chs, dc in next ch, turn.

Row 3: Ch 4, [dc in next dc, ch 1] 4 times; dc in 3rd ch of turning ch-4, turn.

Row 4: Rep row 3.

Row 5: Ch 4, [dc in next dc, ch 1] 4 times; dc in 3rd ch of turning ch-4. Do not turn.

Note: Next part of Motif is worked in a rnd.

Rnd 1: Ch 1, working around edge of piece, 2 sc in each of next 4 sps; *5 sc in next sp—*corner made*; 2 sc in each of next 3 sps; rep from * twice; 3 sc in same sp as beg 2 sc made—*corner made*; join with sl st in first sc.

Note: Remainder of Motif is worked in rows.

Row 1: Ch 1, sc in same sc as joining; ch 1, sl st in next 3 sc; *ch 6, sk next 2 sc, sl st in next 4 sc, ch 1, sc in next sc—*sc corner made*; ch 1, sl st in next 4 sc; rep from* once; ch 6, sk next 2 sc, sl st in next 4 sc, ch 1, sc in next sc—*sc corner made*, turn.

Row 2: Ch 6; *sc in 2nd ch of next ch-6 sp, ch 6, sk next 2 chs, sc in next ch, ch 6, sc in next corner sc, ch 6; rep from * once; sc in 2nd ch of next ch-6 sp, ch 6, sk next 2 chs, sc in next ch, ch 6, sc in next corner sc, turn.

Joining row: Ch 1, 7 sc in next ch-6 sp; 3 sc in next ch-6 sp; ch 1; holding WS of Motif A facing WS of working Motif *(see Sleeve diagram)* and matching sts, sl st in 2nd ch of corresponding corner ch-3 sp on Motif A; *ch 1; on working Motif, 3 sc in same sp as previous sc worked—*joined corner made*; [4 sc in next ch-6 sp, sc around post of 4th sc of corresponding ch-6 sp on Motif A, on working Motif, 3 sc in same sp as previous 3 sc made] twice; 3 sc in next ch-6 sp; ch 1; sl st in center of joining sc of corresponding ch-3 sps on completed Motifs; rep from * once; 4 sc in next ch-6 sp; sc around post of 4th sc of corresponding ch-6 sp on next Motif, on working Motif, 3 sc in same sp as previous 3 sc made. Fasten off.

Motif G

Row 1 (RS): Ch 14; dc in 6th ch from hook *(beg 5 sk chs count as a ch-1 sp, a dc and a ch-1 sp)*, [ch 1, sk next ch, dc in next ch] 4 times, turn.

Row 2: Ch 4 *(counts as a dc on this and following rows)*, [dc in next dc, ch 1] 4 times; sk next ch of beg 5 sk chs, dc in next ch, turn.

Row 3: Ch 4, [dc in next dc, ch 1] 4 times; dc in 3rd ch of turning ch-4, turn.

Row 4: Rep row 3.

Row 5: Ch 4, [dc in next dc, ch 1] 4 times; dc in 3rd ch of turning ch-4. Do not turn.

Note: Next part of Motif is worked in a rnd.

Rnd 1: Ch 1, working around edge of piece, 2 sc in each of next 4 sps; *5 sc in next sp—*corner made*; 2 sc in each of next 3 sps; rep from * twice; 3 sc in same sp as beg 2 sc made—*corner made*; join with sl st in first sc.

Note: Remainder of Motif is worked in rows.

Row 1: Ch 1, sc in same sc as joining; ch 1, sl st in next 3 sc; *ch 6, sk next 2 sc, sl st in next 4 sc, ch 1, sc in next sc—*sc corner made*; ch 1, sl st in next 4 sc; rep from* once; ch 6, sk next 2 sc, sl st in next 4 sc, ch 1, sc in next sc—*sc corner made*, turn.

Row 2: Ch 6; *sc in 2nd ch of next ch-6 sp, ch 6, sk next 2 chs, sc in next ch, ch 6, sc in next corner sc, ch 6; rep from * once; sc in 2nd ch of next ch-6 sp, ch 6, sk next 2 chs, sc in next ch, ch 6, sc in next corner sc, turn.

Joining row: Ch 1, 4 sc in next ch-6 sp; holding WS of Half Motif B facing WS of working Motif *(see Sleeve diagram)* and matching sts, sc around post of 4th sc of corresponding ch-6 sp on Half Motif B, on working Motif, 3 sc in same sp as previous 4 sc made; 3 sc in next ch-6 sp; ch 1, sc in 2nd ch of corresponding ch-3 sp on Motif D, ch 1, on working Motif, 3 sc in same sp as previous sc worked—

joined corner made; [4 sc in next ch-6 sp, sc around post of 4th sc of corresponding ch-6 sp on Motif D, on working Motif, 3 sc in same sp as previous 3 sc made] twice; 3 sc in next ch-6 sp; ch 1; sl st in center of joining sc of corresponding ch-3 sps on completed Motifs; ch 1, on working Motif, 3 sc in same sp as previous sc worked; [4 sc in next sp, sc around post of 4th sc of corresponding ch-6 sp on Motif B, on working Motif, 3 sc in same sp as previous sc worked]

twice; 3 sc in next ch-6 sp, ch 1, sc in 2nd ch of corresponding ch-3 sp on Motif B, ch 1, on working Motif, 3 sc in same sp as previous sc worked; 7 sc in next ch-6 sp. Fasten off.

Assembly

Block pieces if necessary. Sew shoulder seams matching Motif joinings and taking 2 or 3 sts at each joining. Matching center of Sleeves to shoulder seams, sew in Sleeves. Sew side and Sleeve seams.

BABY BLOCKS AFGHAN

Design by Jennine Korejko

Skill Level

EASY

Finished Size

Approximately 34 x 43 inches

Materials

- Fine (sport) weight yarn:
  11 oz/946 yds/308g
  white *(A)*
  2 oz/172 yds/56g each,
  lavender, green, orange, yellow,
  blue, pink *(B)*
- Size F/5/3.75mm crochet hook or
  size needed to obtain gauge
- Tapestry needle

Gauge

9 dc = 2 inches

Special Stitches

Beginning popcorn (beg pc):
Ch 3, 2 dc in st indicated; drop lp
from hook, insert hook in 3rd ch of
beg ch-3, draw dropped lp through.

Popcorn (pc):
3 dc in st; drop lp from hook, insert
hook in first dc made, draw dropped
lp through.

INSTRUCTIONS

Square

Make 64.

Note: Randomly use all colors listed as
B in Materials.

Rnd 1 (RS): With A, ch 5; join with sl st
to form ring; **beg pc** *(see Special Stitches)*
in ring, ch 3, [**pc** *(see Special Stitches)* in
ring, ch 3] 7 times; join in top of beg pc.
(8 ch-3 sps)

Fasten off.

Rnd 2: Join any B in any ch-3 sp; ch 3
(counts as a dc on this and following rnds),
in same sp work (dc, pc, ch 3, pc, 2
dc)—*beg corner made*; 2 dc in next ch-3
sp; *in next ch-3 sp work (2 dc, pc, ch 3,
pc, 2 dc)—*corner made*; 2 dc in next ch-3
sp; rep from * twice; join with sl st in 3rd
ch of beg ch-3. Fasten off.

Rnd 3: Join new B with sl st in any corner ch-3 sp; ch 2 *(counts as a hdc on this and following rnds)*, in same sp work (hdc, ch 3, 2 hdc)—*beg hdc corner made*; hdc in next 8 sts; *in next corner ch-3 sp work (2 hdc, ch 3, 2 hdc)—*hdc corner made*; hdc in next 8 sts; rep from * twice; join with sl st in 2nd ch of beg ch-2. *(48 hdc)*

Fasten off.

Rnd 4: Join new B with sl st in any corner ch-3 sp; in same sp work (beg pc, ch 3, pc)—*beg pc corner made*; ch 3, sk next hdc, pc in next hdc; ch 3, [sk next 2 hdc, pc in next hdc, ch 3] 3 times; sk next hdc; *in next corner ch-3 sp work (pc, ch 3, pc)—*pc corner made*; ch 3, sk next hdc, pc in next hdc; ch 3, [sk next 2 hdc, pc in next hdc, ch 3] 3 times; sk next hdc; rep from * twice; join with sl st in top of beg pc.

Rnd 5: Join A with sl st in any corner ch-3 sp; ch 2, in same sp work (3 dc, hdc)—*beg dc corner made*; 3 hdc in each of next 5 ch-3 sps; *in next corner ch-3 sp work (hdc, 3 dc, hdc)—*dc corner made*; 3 hdc in each of next 5 ch-3 sps; rep from * twice; join with sl st in 2nd ch of beg ch-2.

Fasten off and weave in all ends.

Assembly

Join Squares in 8 rows of 8 Squares each. To join, hold 2 Squares with RS tog. With tapestry needle and A, and working in **back lps** *(see page 28)* only, sew Squares tog, beg and ending in 2nd dc of each corner. Join rem Squares in same manner.

Edging

Rnd 1 (RS): Hold afghan with RS facing you and 1 short end at top; join A in back lp of 2nd dc in upper right-hand corner; ch 3 *(counts as a dc)*, in same sp work (dc, ch 3, 2 dc)—*beg corner made*; working in back lps only, *[dc in next 19 sts, in 2nd dc of joined corner, in joining, and in 2nd dc on next joined corner] 7 times; dc in next 19 sts, in next dc work (2 dc, ch 3, 2 dc)—*corner made*; rep from * twice; [dc in next 19 sts, in 2nd dc of joined corner, in joining, and in 2nd dc on next joined corner] 7 times; dc in next 19 sts; join with sl st in 3rd ch of beg ch-3.

Rnd 2: Sl st in next dc and in next ch-3 sp, ch 1, in same sp work (sc, ch 3, sc)—*sc corner made*; *ch 1, sk next dc, sc in next dc, [ch 3, sk next dc, sc in next dc, ch 1, sk next dc, sc in next dc] 43 times; ch 3, sk next dc, sc in next dc, ch 1, sk next dc, in next ch-3 sp work (sc, ch 3, sc)—*sc corner made*; rep from * twice; ch 1, sk next dc, sc in next dc, [ch 3, sk next dc, sc in next dc, ch 1, sk next dc, sc in next dc] 43 times; ch 3, sk next dc, sc in next st, ch 1, sk next st; join with sl st in first sc.

Rnd 3: Sl st in next ch-3 sp, beg pc in same sp; ch 3, sc in next ch-1 sp, ch 3; *pc in next ch-3 sp; ch 3, sc in next ch-1 sp, ch 3; rep from * around; join with sl st in top of beg pc.

Rnd 4: Sl st in next ch-3 sp, ch 1, 3 sc in same sp; sl st in next sc, 3 sc in next ch-3 sp; ch 1; *3 sc in next ch-3 sp; sl st in next sc, 3 sc in next ch-3 sp, ch 1; rep from * around; join with sl st in first sc.

Fasten off and weave in ends.

INCREASING & DECREASING

Chapter 5

TRIANGLE WRAP

Design by Katherine Eng

Skill Level

EASY

Size

Approximately 66 inches wide x 20 inches long

Materials

- N.Y. Yarns Fiesta bulky (chunky) weight yarn (1¾ oz/65 yds/50g per ball): 5 balls #5 aqua eggplant
- Size N/15/9mm crochet hook or size needed to obtain gauge
- Tapestry needle

Gauge

(Sc, ch 2, sc, ch 2, sc) = 3¼ inches

Special Stitch

Shell:
In st indicated work (2 dc, ch 2, 2 dc).

INSTRUCTIONS

Row 1 (RS): Starting at top edge, ch 146; sc in 2nd ch from hook; *ch 2, sk next 2 chs, sc in next ch; rep from * across, turn. *(49 sc)*

Row 2: Ch 1, sc in first sc; *ch 2, sk next ch-2 sp, sc in next sc; rep from * across, turn.

Row 3: Ch 1, sc in first sc; ***shell** (see Special Stitch)* in next sc; sc in next sc; rep from * across, turn.

Row 4: Sl st in first sc, in next 2 dc and in next ch-2 sp; ch 1, sc in same sp; ch 5, sc in next ch-2 sp; rep from * across, turn.

Row 5: Sl st in first sc and in next 3 chs of next ch-5 sp, ch 1, sc in same sp; *shell in next sc; sc in next ch-5 sp; rep from * across, turn.

Rows 6–25: [Work rows 4 and 5] 10 times.

Row 26: Sl st in first sc, in next 2 dc and in next ch-2 sp; ch 1, sc in same sp; ch 5, sc in next ch-2 sp, turn.

Border

Ch 1, sc in first sc, shell in next ch-5 sp; working across next side, *ch 1, shell in ch-2 sp of next shell, ch 1, sc in next sp; rep from * to last shell; ch 1, shell in ch-2 sp of last shell, ch 1, sc in end of row 2, ch 1, in corner work (shell, ch 1, sc); working across top edge, [sk next 2 chs, shell in next ch; sk next 2 chs, sc in next ch] 24 times; ch 1, shell in same last ch; working across next side, ch 1, sc in end of row 2; *ch 1, shell in ch-2 sp of next shell, ch 1, sc in next sp; rep from * to last shell; ch 1, shell in ch-2 sp of last sc; ch 1; join with sl st in first sc.

Fasten off and weave in ends.

WARM ACCENTS

Designs by Katherine Eng

Skill Level

EASY

Finished Sizes

Hat: one size fits most

Scarf: approximately 4 x 34 inches

Materials

- N.Y. Yarns Misty bulky (chunky) weight yarn (1¾ oz/65 yds/50g per ball): 2 balls #1 *(A)*
- N.Y. Yarns Twinkle bulky (chunky) weight yarn (1¾ oz/92 yds/50g per ball): 2 balls #23 *(B)*
- Sizes I/9/5.5 and N/15/9mm crochet hooks or size needed to obtain gauge
- Tapestry needle

Gauge

Size N hook and 2 strands held tog: 5 dc = 2¼ inches

HAT INSTRUCTIONS

Row 1 (RS): With N hook and 1 strand of A and B held tog, ch 26; dc in 4th ch from hook *(beg 3 sk chs count as a dc)* and in each rem ch, turn. *(24 dc)*

Row 2: Ch 1, working in **back lps** *(see page 28)* only, sc in each dc and in 3rd ch of beg 3 sk chs, turn.

Row 3: Ch 3 *(counts as a dc on this and following rows)*, working in back lps only, dc in each rem sc, turn.

Row 4: Ch 1, working in back lps only, sc in each dc and in 3rd ch of turning ch-3, turn.

Rows 5–24: [Work rows 3 and 4] 10 times.

Fasten off, leaving 12-inch end of B for sewing. Weave in other ends.

Assembly

Hold piece with RS facing you; with tapestry needle and long end, sew unused lps of beg ch and back lps of sc of row 24 tog to form back seam.

Top Section

Rnd 1 (RS): Hold piece with 1 edge at top; with N hook and 1 strand of A and B held tog, join with sl st in end of row 24; ch 1, sc in same sp and in end of each rem row; join with sl st in first sc. *(24 sc)*

Rnd 2: Ch 1, sc in same sc; *ch 1, sk next sc, sc in next sc; rep from * to last sc; ch 1, sk last sc; join with sl st in first sc.

Rnd 3: Sl st in next ch-1 sp, ch 1, sc in same sp and in each rem ch-1 sp; join in first sc. *(12 sc)*

Rnd 4: Rep rnd 2.

Fasten off, leaving 12-inch end of B for sewing. Weave in other ends.

Flower

Rnd 1 (RS): With I hook and B, ch 4; join to form a ring; [ch 4, sl st in ring] 6 times.

Rnd 2: Ch 1, [working behind next ch-4 sp, sc in ring between sl sts, ch 2] 6 times; join in first sc.

Rnd 3: Ch 1, sc in same sc; 5 dc in next ch-2 sp; [sc in next sc, 5 dc in next ch-2 sp] 5 times; join with sl st in first sc.

Fasten off and weave in ends.

Finishing

Step 1: On Hat, with tapestry needle, weave long end through sc of rnd 2. Pull to tighten and secure end. Turn bottom up to form cuff.

Step 2: Referring to photo for placement, sew Flower to Hat over edge of cuff.

SCARF INSTRUCTIONS

Row 1 (RS): With N hook and 1 strand of A and B held tog, ch 62; dc in 4th ch from hook *(beg 3 sk chs count as a dc)* and in each rem ch, turn. *(60 dc)*

Row 2: Ch 1, working in **back lps** *(see page 28)* only, sc in each dc and in 3rd ch of beg 3 sk chs, turn.

Row 3: Ch 3 *(counts as a dc on this and following rows)*, working in back lps only, dc in each rem sc.

Fasten off and weave in all ends.

Border

Rnd 1: Hold piece with RS facing you; with N hook, join 1 strand of B in 3rd ch of beg ch-3 of row 3; ch 1, in same ch as joining work (sc, ch 2, sc)—*corner made*; sc in each dc to last dc; in last dc work (sc, ch 2, sc)—*corner made*; working across next side in ends of rows, sc in each row; working across next side in unused lps of beg ch, in next lp work (sc, ch 2, sc)—*corner made*; sc in each rem lp to last lp; in last lp work (sc, ch 2, sc)—*corner made*; working across next side in ends of rows, sc in each row; join in first sc.

Rnd 2: Sl st in next ch-2 sp, ch 2, sl st in same sp; *ch 2, sl st in next sc; rep from * to next corner; ch 2, in corner ch-2 sp work (sl st, ch 2, sl st); **ch 2, sl st in next sc; rep from ** to next corner; ch 2, in corner ch-2 sp work (sl st, ch 2, sl st); ***ch 2, sl st in next sc; rep from *** to next corner; ch 2, in corner ch-2 sp work (sl st, ch 2, sl st); *****ch 2, sl st in next sc; rep from **** to joining sl st; join in joining sl st.

Fasten off and weave in ends.

Fringe

Cut 14-inch strands of A and B. For each knot of fringe, hold 1 strand of each tog and fold in half. Draw folded end through first ch-2 sp on 1 short end of Scarf. Draw ends through fold and tighten knot. Tie knot in each rem ch-2 sp across each short end of Scarf. Trim ends even.

JUST FOR BABY

Designs by Tamara Gonzales

Skill Level

EASY

Finished Sizes

Instructions given fit child's size 3 months, 6–12 months and 18–24 months. Hook size determines garment finished size. Information for larger sizes is in [ ].

Materials

- DMC Senso Microfiber Cotton yarn (150 yds per ball):
  3 [4, 5] balls #1101 white *(A)*
  small amount of #1104 pink *(B)*
- Size 1/2.25mm steel crochet hook or size needed to obtain gauge (for size 3 months)
- Size 0/2.50mm steel crochet hook or size needed to obtain gauge (for size 6–12 months)
- Size 00/2.70mm steel crochet hook or size needed to obtain gauge (for size 18–24 months)
- Tapestry needle
- 3 light pink ¾-inch buttons
- 1 light pink ⅞-inch button
- Sewing needle and matching thread

Gauge

Size 1 hook: 6 hdc = 1 inch
Size 0 hook: 5 hdc = 1 inch
Size 00 hook: 4 hdc = 1 inch

Special Stitch

Cluster (cl):

Keeping last lp of each tr on hook, tr in 3 sts indicated, yo and draw through all 4 lps on hook.

SWEATER INSTRUCTIONS

Back

Row 1 (RS): With appropriate hook and A, ch 64; hdc in 3rd ch from hook *(beg 2 sk chs count as a hdc)* and in each rem ch, turn. *(63 hdc)*

Row 2: Ch 2 *(counts as a hdc on this and following rows)*, hdc in each rem hdc and in 2nd ch of beg 2 sk chs, turn.

Row 3: Ch 2, hdc in each rem hdc and in 2nd ch of turning ch-2, turn.

Rows 4–18: Rep row 3.

Note: *Join separate strand of A with sl st in turning ch-2 of last row worked; ch 31 for sleeve. Fasten off.*

Row 19: Ch 31, hdc in 3rd ch from hook *(beg 2 sk chs count as a hdc)*, in each rem ch, in each hdc and in each ch, turn. *(123 hdc)*

Row 20: Ch 2, hdc in each rem hdc and in 2nd ch of beg 2 sk chs, turn.

Row 21: Ch 1, sc in first 9 hdc, hdc in next 31 hdc, dc in next 45 hdc, hdc in next 31 hdc, sc in last 7 hdc and in 2nd ch of turning ch-2, turn.

Row 22: Ch 1, sc in first 8 sc, hdc in next 31 sts, dc in next 45 sts, hdc in next 31 sts, sc in last 8 sc, turn.

Row 23: Ch 1, sc in first 8 sc, hdc in next 31 sts, dc in next 45 sts, hdc in next 31 sts, sc in last 8 sc, turn.

Rows 24–35 [Work rows 22 and 23] 6 times.

Row 36: Ch 1, sc in first 8 sc, hdc in next 16 sts, dc in next 9 sts, tr in next 21 sts, dc in next 16 sts, tr in next 21 sts, dc in next 9 sts, hdc in next 15 sts, sc in last 8 sc, turn.

Neck & Right Front Shaping

Row 1: Ch 1, sc in first 8 sc, hdc in next 18 sts, dc in next 24 sts, tr in next st, **tr dec** *(see page 25)* in next 2 sts, turn, leaving rem sts unworked. *(52 sts)*

Row 2: Ch 3, dc in next 25 sts, hdc in next 18 sts, sc in last 8 sc, turn.

Row 3: Ch 1, sc in first 8 sc, hdc in next 18 sts, dc in next 25 sts and in 3rd ch of turning ch-3, turn.

Row 4: Ch 3, dc in first dc and in next 25 sts, hdc in next 18 sts, sc in last 8 sc, turn. *(53 sts)*

Row 5: Ch 1, sc in first 8 sc, hdc in next 18 sts, dc in next 26 sts, 2 dc in 3rd ch of turning ch-3, turn. *(54 sts)*

Row 6: Ch 21, dc in 4th ch from hook *(beg 3 sk chs count as a dc)* and in next 44 sts, hdc in next 19 sts, sc in last 8 sc, turn. *(73 sts)*

Row 7: Ch 1, sc in first 8 sc, hdc in next 19 sts, dc in next 45 sts and in 3rd ch of beg 3 sk chs, turn.

Row 8: Ch 3, dc in next 45 sts, hdc in next 19 sts, sc in last 8 sc, turn.

Row 9: Ch 1, sc in first 8 sc, hdc in next 64 sts and in 3rd ch of turning ch-3, turn.

Row 10: Ch 2, hdc in next 64 sts, sc in last 8 sc, turn.

Rows 11–18: [Work rows 9 and 10] 4 times.

Fasten off and weave in all ends.

Lower Front Section

Row 1 (RS): Hold piece with RS facing you; sk first 30 sts; with appropriate hook, join A with sl st in next hdc; ch 2 *(counts as a hdc on this and following rows)*, hdc in each rem hdc and in 2nd ch of turning ch-2, turn. *(42 sts)*

Row 2: Ch 2, hdc in each rem hdc and in 2nd ch of beg ch-2, turn.

Row 3: Ch 2, hdc in each rem hdc and in 2nd ch of turning ch-2, turn.

Rows 4–19: Rep row 3.

Fasten off and weave in ends.

Neck & Left Front Shaping

Row 1: Sk center back 19 hdc; with appropriate hook, join A with sl st in next hdc; ch 4 *(counts as a tr)*, tr in next st, dc in next 23 sts, hdc in next 18 sts, sc in last 8 sc, turn. *(51 sts)*

Row 2: Ch 1, sc in first 8 sc, hdc in next 18 sts, dc in next 24 sts and in 4th ch of beg ch-4, turn.

Row 3: Ch 3, dc in first dc and in next 24 sts, hdc in next 18 sts, sc in last 8 sc, turn.

Row 4: Ch 1, sc in first 8 sc, hdc in next 18 sts, dc in next 25 [25, 25] sts, 2 dc in 3rd ch of turning ch-3, turn. *(53 sts)*

Row 5: Ch 3, dc in next 26 sts, hdc in next 18 sts, sc in last 8 sc, turn.

Row 6: Ch 1, sc in first 8 sc, hdc in next 18 sts, dc in next 26 sts and in 3rd ch of turning ch-3, tr in base of dc just made, tr in base of tr just made, tr in base of tr just made, turn. *(56 sts)*

Row 7: Ch 3, dc in next 29 sts, hdc in next 18 sts, sc in last 8 sc, turn.

Row 8: Ch 1, sc in first 8 sc, hdc in next 18 sts, dc in last 29 sts and in 3rd ch of turning ch-3, turn.

Row 9: Ch 2, hdc in next 47 sts, sc in last 8 sc, turn.

Row 10: Ch 1, sc in first 8 sc, hdc in next 47 sts and in 2nd ch of turning ch-2, turn.

Row 11: Ch 2, hdc in next 47 sts, sc in last 8 sc, turn.

Row 12: Ch 1, sc in first 8 sc, hdc in next 47 sts and in 2nd ch of turning ch-2.

Rows 13–18: [Work rows 11 and 12] 3 times.

Row 19: Ch 2, hdc in next 24 sts, turn, leaving rem sts unworked.

Row 20: Ch 2, hdc in next 23 sts and in 2nd ch of turning ch-2.

Rows 21–36: Rep row 20.

Fasten off and weave in ends.

Assembly

With RS tog sew side seams.

Edgings

Body Edging

Hold Sweater with RS facing you and lower edge at top; with appropriate hook, join B in 1 side seam; ch 1, sc in same sp; sc evenly spaced around outer end, working 2 or 3 sc around corners and dec 1 or 2 sc at curves; join in first sc.

Fasten off and weave in ends.

Sleeve Edging

Hold 1 Sleeve with RS facing you and lower edge at top; with appropriate hook, join B in seam; ch 1, sc in same sp; sc evenly spaced around edge; join in first sc.

Fasten off and weave in ends.

Rep on other Sleeve.

Button Loops

Make 3.

With appropriate hook and B, ch 16; sc in 2nd ch from hook and in each rem ch.

Fasten off and weave in ends.

Finishing

Referring to photo for placement, sew Button Lps to Right Front. Sew ¾-inch buttons on Left Front opposite Lps.

HAT INSTRUCTIONS

Rnd 1: With appropriate hook and A, ch 6; join with sl st to form ring, ch 1, 14 sc in ring; join in first sc. *(14 sc)*

Rnd 2: Ch 4 *(counts as a dc and a ch-1 sp)*; *dc in next sc, ch 1; rep from * around; join with sl st in 3rd ch of beg ch-4. *(14 ch-1 sps)*

Rnd 3: Ch 2 *(counts as a hdc on this and following rnds)*; *2 hdc in next ch-1 sp; hdc in next dc, hdc in next ch-1 sp, hdc in next dc; rep from * 5 times; 2 hdc in next ch-1 sp; hdc in next dc, hdc in next ch-1 sp, join with sl st in 2nd ch of beg ch-2. *(35 hdc)*

Rnd 4: Ch 2; *2 hdc in next hdc, hdc in next hdc, rep from * around; join with sl st in 2nd ch of beg ch-2. *(52 hdc)*

Rnd 5: Ch 2, hdc in each rem hdc; join with sl st in 2nd ch of beg ch-2.

Rnd 6: Rep rnd 5.

Rnd 7: Ch 2; *hdc in next 4 hdc, 2 hdc in next hdc; rep from * to last hdc; hdc in last hdc; join with sl st in 2nd ch of turning ch-2. *(62 hdc)*

Rnds 8 & 9: Rep rnd 5.

Rnd 10: Ch 2, hdc in next 4 hdc, 2 hdc in next hdc; *hdc in next 5 hdc, 2 hdc in next hdc; rep from * to last 2 hdc; hdc in last 2 hdc; join with sl st in 2nd ch of turning ch-2. *(72 hdc)*

Rnd 11: Ch 2, hdc in next 4 hdc, 2 hdc in next hdc; *hdc in next 5 hdc, 2 hdc in next hdc; rep from * around; join with sl st in 2nd ch of turning ch-2. *(84 hdc)*

Rnds 12–17: Rep rnd 5.

Rnd 18: Ch 2, hdc in each rem hdc; join with sl st in 2nd ch of beg ch-2, turn.

Rnd 19: Ch 3 *(counts as a dc)*, dc in each rem hdc; join in 3rd ch of beg ch-3.

Rnd 20: Ch 1, sc in same ch as joining; ch 4, sk next 2 dc; *sc in next dc, ch 4, sk next 2 dc; rep from * around; join with sl st in first sc. *(28 ch-4 sps)*

Rnd 21: Sl st in next ch-4 sp; ch 1, sc in same sp, ch 1, 7 dc in next ch-1 sp; ch 1; *sc in next ch-4 sp, ch 1, 7 dc in next ch-4 sp; ch 1; rep from * around; join with sl st in first sc.

Fasten off and weave in ends.

Flower

Rnd 1: With appropriate hook and B, ch 5; join with sl st to form ring, ch 3 *(counts as a dc)*, 14 dc in ring; join with sl st in 3rd ch of beg ch-3. *(15 dc)*

Rnd 2: Ch 3, in same ch as joining work (2 dc, ch 3, sl st); in each rem dc work (sl st, ch 3, 2 dc, ch 3, sl st); join with sl st in joining sl st.

Fasten off and weave in ends.

Finishing

Sew Flower to brim of Hat and sew ⅞-inch button to center of Flower.

COLORFUL TABLE SET

Designs by Maria Merlino

Skill Level

EASY

Size

Approximately 20 x 15 inches

Materials (for one placemat and napkin ring)

- Lily Sugar 'n Cream medium (worsted) weight cotton yarn (2 oz/95 yds/56g per ball):
  2 balls #2743 summer splash
- Sizes H/8/5mm and I/9/5.5mm crochet hooks or size needed to obtain gauge
- Tapestry needle

Gauge

Size H hook: 7 dc = 2 inches

Special Stitches

Beginning shell (beg shell):
Ch 3, 2 dc in sp indicated.

Shell:
3 dc in sp indicated.

INSTRUCTIONS

Placemat

First Half

Row 1 (RS): With I hook, ch 60; change to H hook; **shell** *(see Special Stitches)* in 3rd ch from hook; *sk next 2 chs, shell in next ch; rep from * across, turn. *(20 shells)*

Row 2: Ch 1, sk first dc, sl st in next 2 dc and in sp between first 2 shells, **beg shell** *(see Special Stitches)* in same sp; * shell in sp between next 2 shells, rep from * across, turn. *(19 shells)*

Row 3: Ch 1, sk first dc, sl st in next 2 dc and in sp between first 2 shells, beg shell in same sp; * shell in sp between next 2 shells, rep from * across, turn. *(18 shells)*

Rows 4–15: Rep row 3. *(6 shells at end of row 15)*

Row 16: Sk first dc, sl st in next 2 dc and in sp between first 2 shells, beg shell in same sp; shell in sp first 2 shells; [shell in sp between next 2 shells] twice; in sp between last 2 shells work (2 dc, ch 3, sl st). *(5 shells)*

Fasten off and weave in ends.

2nd Half

Row 1: Hold piece with beg ch at top; join yarn with sl st in first sp formed sk chs of beg ch; beg shell in same sp; * shell in sp between next 2 shells, rep from * across, turn. *(19 shells)*

Row 2: Ch 1, sk first dc, sl st in next 2 dc and in sp between first 2 shells, beg shell in same sp; * shell in sp between next 2 shells, rep from * across, turn. *(18 shells)*

Rows 3–15: Rep row 2. *(6 shells at end of row 15)*

Row 16: Sk first dc, sl st in next 2 dc and in sp between first 2 shells, beg shell in same sp; shell in sp first 2 shells; [shell in sp between next 2 shells] twice; in sp between last 2 shells work (2 dc, ch 3, sl st). *(5 shells)*

Fasten off and weave in all ends.

Napkin Ring

Rnd 1: With H hook, ch 20; join with sl st to form ring; ch 1, 5 sc in ring; join with sl st in first sc—*base of flower made.*

Rnd 3: Ch 1, 3 sc in same sc as joining and in each rem sc; join with sl st in first sc. *(15 sc)*

Rnd 4: Ch 1, 3 sc in same sc and in each rem sc; join with sl st in first sc. *(45 sc)*

Fasten off and weave in all ends.

COMFY STRIPES CARDIGAN

Design by Svetlana Avrakh

Skill Level

EASY

Finished Sizes

Instructions given fit woman's size small; changes for medium, large, X-large and 2/3X-large are in [ ].

Finished Garment Measurements

Chest: 39¾ inches (*small*) [42½ inches (*medium*), 46 inches (*large*), 50 inches (*X-large*), 57 inches (*2/3X-large*)]

Materials for Adult

- Patons Classic Merino Wool medium (worsted) weight yarn (3½ oz/223 yds/100g per ball):
  2 [2, 2, 2, 3] balls #00208 burgundy (A)
  2 [2, 2, 2, 3] balls #00205 deep olive (B)
  2 [2, 2, 2, 3] balls #00206 russet (C)
  2 [2, 2, 2, 3] balls #00212 royal purple (D)
- Size H/8/5mm crochet hook or size needed to obtain gauge
- Tapestry needle
- Stitch markers
- 6 matching 1-inch buttons
- Sewing needle and matching thread

For girl's cardigan, see page 91.

Gauge

13 dc = 4 inches

Patten Note

To change color, work last stitch until 2 loops remain on hook; with new color, yarn over and draw through 2 loops on hook. Cut old color.

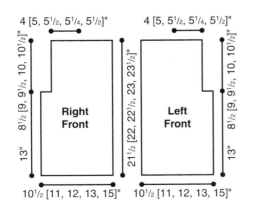

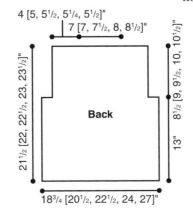

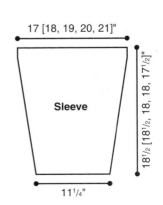

INSTRUCTIONS (for adult)

Back

Row 1 (RS): With A, ch 63 [69, 75, 81, 90]; dc in 4th ch from hook (*beg 3 sk chs count as a dc*) and in each rem ch, changing to B in last dc; cut A, turn. (*61 [67, 73, 79, 88] dc*)

Row 2: Ch 1, sc in first dc; *ch 3, sk next 2 dc, sc in next dc; rep from * last 2 dc and beg 3 sk chs; ch 3, sk last 2 dc, sc in 3rd ch of beg 3 sk chs, turn.

Row 3: Ch 3 (*counts as a dc on this and following rows*); *2 dc in next ch-3 sp; dc in next sc; rep from * across, changing to C in last dc; cut B, turn.

Row 4: Ch 1, sc in first dc; *ch 3, sk next 2 dc, sc in next dc; rep from * last 2 dc and turning ch-3; ch 3, sk last 2 dc, sc in 3rd ch of turning ch-3, turn.

Row 5: Ch 3; *2 dc in next ch-3 sp; dc in next sc; rep from * across, changing to D in last dc; cut C, turn.

Rows 6 & 7: Rep rows 4 and 5. At end of row 7, change to A in last dc; cut D.

Rows 8 & 9: Rep rows 4 and 5. At end of row 9, change to B in last dc; cut A.

Rows 10 & 11: Rep rows 4 and 5. At end of row 11, change to C in last dc; cut B.

Rep rows 4–11 until piece measures 13 inches from beg, ending with a RS row.

Fasten off and weave in all ends.

Armhole Shaping

Note: *Work rem rows in same color sequence.*

Row 1 (WS): Hold piece with WS facing you; sk first 6 [6, 6, 9, 12] dc; join appropriate color with sl st in next dc; ch 1, sc in same dc; *ch 3, sk next 2 dc, sc in next dc; rep from * to last 5 [5, 5, 8, 11] dc and turning ch-3, turn, leaving rem dc and turning ch-3 unworked.

Row 2 (RS): Ch 3; *2 dc in next ch-3 sp; dc in next sc; rep from * across, changing to next color in last dc; cut old color, turn.

Row 3: Ch 1, sc in first dc; *ch 3, sk next 2 dc, sc in next dc; rep from * to last 2 dc and turning ch-3; ch 3, sk last 2 dc, sc in 3rd ch of turning ch-3, turn.

Rep rows 2 and 3 until armhole measures 8½ [9, 9½, 10, 10½] inches, ending with a RS row.

Fasten off and weave in all ends.

Note: *Place markers 13 [16, 18, 17, 18] dc in from side edges for shoulders.*

Right Front

Row 1 (RS): With A, ch 36 [39, 42, 45, 51]; dc in 4th ch from hook (*beg 3 sk chs count as a dc*) and in each rem ch, changing to B in last dc; cut A, turn. (*34 [37, 40, 43, 49] dc*)

Row 2: Ch 1, sc in first dc; *ch 3, sk next 2 dc, sc in next dc; rep from * last 2 dc and beg 3 sk chs; ch 3, sk last 2 dc, sc in 3rd ch of beg 3 sk chs, turn.

Row 3: Ch 3 (*counts as a dc on this and following rows*); *2 dc in next ch-3 sp; dc in next sc; rep from * across, changing to C in last dc; cut B, turn.

Row 4: Ch 1, sc in first dc; *ch 3, sk next 2 dc, sc in next dc; rep from * last 2 dc and turning ch-3; ch 3, sk last 2 dc, sc in 3rd ch of turning ch-3, turn.

Row 5: Ch 3; *2 dc in next ch-3 sp; dc in next sc; rep from * across, changing to D in last dc; cut C, turn.

Rows 6 & 7: Rep rows 4 and 5. At end of row 7, change to A in last dc; cut D.

Rows 8 & 9: Rep rows 4 and 5. At end of row 9, change to B in last dc; cut A.

Rows 10 & 11: Rep rows 4 and 5. At end of row 11, change to C in last dc; cut B.

Rep rows 4–11 until piece measures 13 inches from beg, ending with a RS row. Fasten off.

Armhole Shaping

Note: *Work rem rows in same color sequence.*

Row 1 (WS): Hold piece with WS facing you; sk first 6 [6, 9, 9, 12] dc; join appropriate color in next dc; ch 1, sc in same dc; *ch 3, sk next 2 dc, sc in next dc; rep from * to last 2 dc and turning ch-3; ch 3, sk last 2 dc, sc in 3rd ch of turning ch-3, turn.

Row 2 (RS): Ch 3; *2 dc in next ch-3 sp; dc in next sc; rep from * across, changing to next color in last dc; cut old color, turn.

Row 3: Ch 1, sc in first dc; *ch 3, sk next 2 dc, sc in next dc; rep from * to last 2 dc and turning ch-3; ch 3, sk last 2 dc, sc in 3rd ch of turning ch-3, turn.

Rep rows 2 and 3 until armhole measures 8½ [9, 9½, 10, 10½] inches, ending with a RS row.

Fasten off and weave in all ends.

Left Front

Work same as Right Front to Armhole Shaping.

Armhole Shaping

Note: *Work rem rows in same color sequence.*

Row 1 (WS): Hold piece with WS facing you; join appropriate color in first dc; ch 1, sc in same dc; *ch 3, sk next 2 dc, sc in next dc; rep from * to last 5 [5, 5, 8, 11] dc and turning ch-3, turn, leaving rem dc and turning ch-3 unworked.

Row 2 (RS): Ch 3; *2 dc in next ch-3 sp; dc in next sc; rep from * across, changing to next color in last dc; cut old color, turn.

Row 3: Ch 1, sc in first dc; *ch 3, sk next 2 dc, sc in next dc; rep from * to last 2 dc and turning ch-3; ch 3, sk last 2 dc, sc in 3rd ch of turning ch-3, turn.

Rep rows 2 and 3 until armhole measures 8½ [9, 9½, 10, 10½] inches, ending with a RS row.

Fasten off and weave in all ends.

Sleeve
Make 2.

Row 1 (RS): With A, ch 39; dc in 4th ch from hook *(beg 3 sk chs count as a dc)* and in each rem ch, changing to B in last dc; cut A, turn. *(37 dc)*

Row 2: Ch 1, sc in first dc; *ch 3, sk next 2 dc, sc in next dc; rep from * to last 2 dc and 3 beg sk chs; ch 3, sk last 2 dc, sc in 3rd ch of beg 3 sk chs, turn.

Row 3: Ch 3 *(counts as a dc on this and following rows)*, dc in first sc; *2 dc in next ch-3 sp; dc in next sc; rep from * to last ch-3 sp; 2 dc in last ch-3 sp; 2 dc in last sc, changing to C in last dc; cut B, turn. *(39 dc)*

Row 4: Ch 1, sc in first 2 dc; *ch 3, sk next 2 dc, sc in next dc; rep from * to turning ch-3; sc in 3rd ch of turning ch-3, turn.

Row 5: Ch 3, dc in first sc and in next sc; *2 dc in next ch-3 sp, dc in next sc; rep from * to last 2 sc; dc in next sc, 2 dc in last sc, changing to D in last dc; cut C, turn. *(41 dc)*

Row 6: Ch 1, sc in first 3 dc; *ch 3, sk next 2 dc, sc in next dc; rep from * to last dc and turning ch-3; sc in last dc and in 3rd ch of turning ch-3, turn.

Row 7: Ch 3, dc in first 3 sc; *2 dc in next ch-3 sp; dc in next sc; rep from * to last 2 sc; dc in next sc, 2 dc in last sc, changing to A in last dc; cut D, turn. *(43 dc)*

Row 8: Ch 1, sc in first dc; *ch 3, sk next 2 dc, sc in next dc; rep from * to last 2 dc and turning ch-3; ch 3, sk last 2 dc, sc in 3rd ch turning ch-3, turn.

Row 9: Ch 3; *2 dc in next ch-3 sp; dc in next sc; rep from * across, changing to B in last dc; cut A, turn.

Row 10: Ch 1, sc in first dc; *ch 3, sk next 2 dc, sc in next dc; rep from * to last 2 dc and turning ch-3; ch 3, sk last 2 dc, sc in 3rd ch of turning ch-3, turn.

Row 11: Ch 3, dc in first sc; *2 dc in next ch-3 sp; dc in next sc; rep from * to last ch-3 sp; 2 dc in last ch-3 sp; 2 dc in last sc, changing to C in last dc; cut B, turn. *(45 dc)*

For Size Small Only

Rows 12–27: [Work rows 4–11] twice. *(57 dc at end of row 27)*

Continue with For All Sizes.

For Size Medium Only

Rows 12–27: [Work rows 4–11] twice. *(57 dc at end of row 27)*

Rows 28 & 29: Rep rows 4 and 5. *(59 dc at end of row 29)*

Continue with For All Sizes.

For Size Large Only

Rows 12–35: [Work rows 4–11] 3 times. *(63 dc at end of row 35)*

Continue with For All Sizes.

For Size X-Large Only

Rows 12–35: [Work rows 4–11] 3 times. *(63 dc at end of row 35)*

Rows 36 & 37: Rep rows 4 and 5. *(65 dc at end of row 37)*

Continue with For All Sizes.

For Size 2/3X-Large Only

Rows 12–43: [Work rows 4–11] 4 times. *(69 dc at end of row 43)*

Continue with For All Sizes.

For All Sizes
Note: Work rem rows in same color sequence.

Row 28 [30, 36, 38, 44]: Ch 1, sc in first dc; *ch 3, sk next 2 dc, sc in next dc; rep from * to last 2 dc and turning ch-3; ch 3, sk last 2 dc, sc in 3rd ch turning ch-3, turn.

Row 29 [31, 37, 39, 45]: Ch 3; *2 dc in next ch-3 sp; dc in next sc; rep from * across, changing to next color in last dc; cut old color, turn.

Rep last 2 rows until piece measures 18½ [18½, 18, 18, 17½] inches from beg, ending with RS row.

Fasten off and weave in all ends.

Assembly
Sew shoulder seams to markers. Sew in Sleeves. Sew side and Sleeve seams.

Edging
Hold Cardigan with RS facing you and Right Front edge at top; join A with sl st in end of row 1 of Right Front; ch 1, sc in same sp; working around outer edge of Cardigan, sc evenly spaced to first sc; join with sl st in first sc.

Fasten off and weave in ends.

Finishing
Step 1: Fold upper corners of Fronts to form lapels. To secure lapels to Fronts, with sewing needle and matching thread, sew 1 button to corner of each lapel.

Step 2: Sew rem buttons to Left Front, having top button at beg of lapel shaping, bottom button 1 inch from lower edge, and rem 2 buttons spaced evenly between.

GIRL'S COMFY STRIPES CARDIGAN

Design by Svetlana Avrakh

Skill Level

EASY

Finished Sizes

Instructions given fit girl's size 4; changes for sizes 6, 8, 10 and 12 are in [ ].

Finished Garment Measurements

Chest: 28½ [29, 32, 33, 36] inches

Materials

- Patons Classic Merino Wool medium (worsted) weight yarn (3½ oz/223 yds/100g per ball): 1 [1, 1, 2, 2] balls #00208 burgundy *(A)* 1 [1, 1, 2, 2] balls #00205 deep olive *(B)* 1 [1, 1, 2, 2] balls #00206 russet *(C)* 1 [1, 1, 2, 2] balls #00212 royal purple *(D)*
- Size H/8/5mm crochet hook or size needed to obtain gauge
- Tapestry needle
- Stitch markers
- 5 matching 1-inch buttons
- Sewing needle and matching thread

Gauge

13 dc = 4 inches

Patten Note

To change color, work last stitch until 2 loops remain on hook; with new color, yarn over and draw through 2 loops on hook. Cut old color.

INSTRUCTIONS

Back

Row 1 (RS): With A, ch 45 [48, 51, 54, 57]; dc in 4th ch from hook *(beg 3 sk chs count as a dc)* and in each rem ch, changing to B in last dc; cut A, turn. *(43 [46, 49, 52, 55] dc)*

Row 2: Ch 1, sc in first dc; *ch 3, sk next 2 dc, sc in next dc; rep from * last 2 dc and beg 3 sk chs; ch 3, sk last 2 dc, sc in 3rd ch of beg 3 sk chs, turn.

Row 3: Ch 3 *(counts as a dc on this and following rows)*; *2 dc in next ch-3 sp; dc in next sc; rep from * across, changing to C in last dc; cut B, turn.

Row 4: Ch 1, sc in first dc; *ch 3, sk next 2 dc, sc in next dc; rep from * last 2 dc and turning ch-3; ch 3, sk last 2 dc, sc in 3rd ch of turning ch-3, turn.

Row 5: Ch 3; *2 dc in next ch-3 sp; dc in next sc; rep from * across, changing to D in last dc; cut C, turn.

Rows 6 & 7: Rep rows 4 and 5. At end of row 7, change to A in last dc; cut D.

Rows 8 & 9: Rep rows 4 and 5. At end of row 9, change to B in last dc; cut A.

Rows 10 & 11: Rep rows 4 and 5. At end of row 11, change to C in last dc; cut B.

Rep rows 4–11 until piece measures 7 [8½, 9½, 10½, 12] inches from beg, ending with a RS row.

Fasten off and weave in all ends.

Armhole Shaping

Note: Work rem rows in same color sequence.

Row 1 (WS): Hold piece with WS facing you; sk first 3 [3, 3, 6, 6] dc; join appropriate color with sl st in next dc; ch 1, sc in same dc; *ch 3, sk next 2 dc, sc in next dc; rep from * to last 2 [2, 2, 5, 5] dc and turning ch-3, turn, leaving rem dc and turning ch-3 unworked.

Row 2 (RS): Ch 3; *2 dc in next ch-3 sp; dc in next sc; rep from * across, changing to next color in last dc; cut old color, turn.

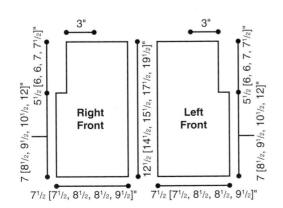

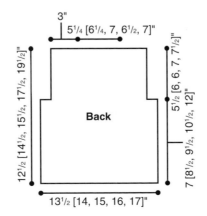

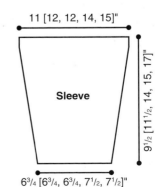

Row 3: Ch 1, sc in first dc; *ch 3, sk next 2 dc, sc in next dc; rep from * to last 2 dc and turning ch-3; ch 3, sk last 2 dc, sc in 3rd ch of turning ch-3, turn.

Rep rows 2 and 3 until armhole measures 5½ [6, 6, 7, 7½] inches, ending with a RS row.

Fasten off and weave in all ends.

Note: Place markers 10 [10, 11, 10, 10] dc in from side edges for shoulders.

Right Front

Row 1 (RS): With A, ch 27 [27, 30, 30, 33]; dc in 4th ch from hook *(beg 3 sk chs count as a dc)* and in each rem ch, changing to B in last dc; cut A, turn. *(25 [25, 28, 28, 31] dc)*

Row 2: Ch 1, sc in first dc; *ch 3, sk next 2 dc, sc in next dc; rep from * last 2 dc and beg 3 sk chs; ch 3, sk last 2 dc, sc in 3rd ch of beg 3 sk chs, turn.

Row 3: Ch 3 *(counts as a dc on this and following rows)*; *2 dc in next ch-3 sp; dc in next sc; rep from * across, changing to C in last dc; cut B, turn.

Row 4: Ch 1, sc in first dc; *ch 3, sk next 2 dc, sc in next dc; rep from * last 2 dc and turning ch-3; ch 3, sk last 2 dc, sc in 3rd ch of turning ch-3, turn.

Row 5: Ch 3; *2 dc in next ch-3 sp; dc in next sc; rep from * across, changing to D in last dc; cut C, turn.

Rows 6 & 7: Rep rows 4 and 5. At end of row 7, change to A in last dc; cut D.

Rows 8 & 9: Rep rows 4 and 5. At end of row 9, change to B in last dc; cut A.

Rows 10 & 11: Rep rows 4 and 5. At end of row 11, change to C in last dc; cut B.

Rep rows 4–11 until piece measures 7 [8½, 9½, 10½, 12] inches from beg, ending with a RS row. Fasten off.

Armhole Shaping

Note: Work rem rows in same color sequence.

Row 1 (WS): Hold piece with WS facing you; sk first 3 [3, 3, 6, 6] dc; join appropriate color in next dc; ch 1, sc in same dc; *ch 3, sk next 2 dc, sc in next dc; rep from * to last 2 dc and turning ch-3; ch 3, sk last 2 dc, sc in 3rd ch of turning ch-3, turn.

Row 2 (RS): Ch 3; *2 dc in next ch-3 sp; dc in next sc; rep from * across, changing to next color in last dc; cut old color, turn.

Row 3: Ch 1, sc in first dc; *ch 3, sk next 2 dc, sc in next dc; rep from * to last 2 dc and turning ch-3; ch 3, sk last 2 dc, sc in 3rd ch of turning ch-3, turn.

Rep rows 2 and 3 until armhole measures 5½ [6, 6, 7, 7½] inches, ending with a RS row.

Fasten off and weave in all ends.

Left Front

Work same as Right Front to Armhole Shaping.

Armhole Shaping

Note: Work rem rows in same color sequence.

Row 1 (WS): Hold piece with WS facing you; join appropriate color in first dc; ch 1, sc in same dc; *ch 3, sk next 2 dc, sc in next dc; rep from * to last 2 [2, 2, 5, 5] dc and turning ch-3, turn, leaving rem dc and turning ch-3 unworked.

Row 2 (RS): Ch 3; *2 dc in next ch-3 sp; dc in next sc; rep from * across, changing to next color in last dc; cut old color, turn.

Row 3: Ch 1, sc in first dc; *ch 3, sk next 2 dc, sc in next dc; rep from * to last 2 dc and turning ch-3; ch 3, sk last 2 dc, sc in 3rd ch of turning ch-3, turn.

Rep rows 2 and 3 until armhole measures 5½ [6, 6, 7, 7½] inches, ending with a RS row.

Fasten off and weave in all ends.

Sleeve
Make 2.

Row 1 (RS): With A, ch 24 (24, 24, 27, 27]; dc in 4th ch from hook *(beg 3 sk chs count as a dc)* and in each rem ch, changing to B in last dc; cut A, turn. *(22 [22, 22, 25, 25] dc)*

Row 2: Ch 1, sc in first dc; *ch 3, sk next 2 dc, sc in next dc; rep from * to last 2 dc and 3 beg sk chs; ch 3, sk last 2 dc, sc in 3rd ch of beg 3 sk chs, turn.

Row 3: Ch 3 *(counts as a dc on this and following rows)*, dc in first sc; *2 dc in next ch-3 sp; dc in next sc; rep from * to last ch-3 sp; 2 dc in last ch-3 sp; 2 dc in last sc, changing to C in last dc; cut B, turn. *(24 [24, 24, 27, 27] dc)*

Row 4: Ch 1, sc in first 2 dc; *ch 3, sk next 2 dc, sc in next dc; rep from * to turning ch-3; sc in 3rd ch of turning ch-3, turn.

Row 5: Ch 3, dc in first sc and in next sc; *2 dc in next ch-3 sp, dc in next sc; rep from * to last 2 sc; dc in next sc, 2 dc in last sc, changing to D in last dc; cut C, turn. *(26 [26, 26, 29, 29] dc)*

Row 6: Ch 1, sc in first 3 dc; *ch 3, sk next 2 dc, sc in next dc; rep from * to last dc and turning ch-3; sc in last dc and in 3rd ch of turning ch-3, turn.

Row 7: Ch 3, dc in first 3 sc; *2 dc in next ch-3 sp; dc in next sc; rep from * to last 2 sc; dc in next sc, 2 dc in last sc, changing to A in last dc; cut D, turn. *(28 [28, 28, 31, 31] dc)*

Row 8: Ch 1, sc in first dc; *ch 3, sk next 2 dc, sc in next dc; rep from * to last 2 dc and turning ch-3; ch 3, sk last 2 dc, sc in 3rd ch turning ch-3, turn.

For Size 4 Only

Row 9: Rep row 3, changing to B in last dc; cut A, turn. *(30 dc)*

Row 10: Rep row 4.

Row 11: Rep row 5, changing to C in last dc; cut B, turn. *(32 dc)*

Row 12: Rep row 6.

Row 13: Rep row 7, changing to D in last dc; cut C, turn. *(34 dc)*

Row 14: Rep row 8.

Row 15: Rep row 3, changing to A in last dc; cut D, turn. *(36 dc)*

Continue with For All Sizes.

For Size 6 Only

Row 9: Rep row 3, changing to B in last dc; cut A, turn. *(30 dc)*

Row 10: Rep row 4.

Row 11: Rep row 5, changing to C in last dc; cut B, turn. *(32 dc)*

Row 12: Rep row 6.

Row 13: Rep row 7, changing to D in last dc; cut C, turn. *(34 dc)*

Row 14: Rep row 8.

Row 15: Rep row 3, changing to A in last dc; cut D, turn. *(36 dc)*

Row 16: Rep row 4.

Row 17: Rep row 5, changing to B in last dc; cut A, turn. *(38 dc)*

Row 18: Rep row 6.

Row 19: Rep row 7, changing to C in last dc; cut B, turn. *(40 dc)*

For Size 8 Only

Row 9: Rep row 3, changing to B in last dc; cut A, turn. *(30 dc)*

Row 10: Rep row 4.

Row 11: Rep row 5, changing to C in last dc; cut B, turn. *(32 dc)*

Row 12: Rep row 6.

Row 13: Rep row 7, changing to D in last dc; cut C, turn. *(34 dc)*

Row 14: Rep row 8.

Row 15: Rep row 3, changing to A in last dc; cut D, turn. *(36 dc)*

Row 16: Rep row 4.

Row 17: Rep row 5, changing to B in last dc; cut A, turn. *(38 dc)*

Row 18: Rep row 6.

Row 19: Rep row 7, changing to C in last dc; cut B, turn. *(40 dc)*

For Size 10 Only

Row 9: Rep row 3, changing to B in last dc; cut A, turn. *(33 dc)*

Row 10: Rep row 4.

Row 11: Rep row 5, changing to C in last dc; cut B, turn. *(35 dc)*

Row 12: Rep row 6.

Row 13: Rep row 7, changing to D in last dc; cut C, turn. *(37 dc)*

Row 14: Rep row 8.

Row 15: Rep row 3, changing to A in last dc; cut D, turn. *(39 dc)*

Row 16: Rep row 4.

Row 17: Rep row 5, changing to B in last dc; cut A, turn. *(41 dc)*

Row 18: Rep row 6.

Row 19: Rep row 7, changing to C in last dc; cut B, turn. *(43 dc)*

Row 20: Rep row 8.

Row 21: Rep row 3, changing to D in last dc; cut C, turn. *(45 dc)*

Continue with For All Sizes.

For Size 12 Only

Row 9: Rep row 3, changing to B in last dc; cut A, turn. *(33 dc)*

Row 10: Rep row 4.

Row 11: Rep row 5, changing to C in last dc; cut B, turn. *(35 dc)*

Row 12: Rep row 6.

Row 13: Rep row 7, changing to D in last dc; cut C, turn. *(37 dc)*

Row 14: Rep row 8.

Row 15: Rep row 3, changing to A in last dc; cut D, turn. *(39 dc)*

Row 16: Rep row 4.

Row 17: Rep row 5, changing to B in last dc; cut A, turn. *(41 dc)*

Row 18: Rep row 6.

Row 19: Rep row 7, changing to C in last dc; cut B, turn. *(43 dc)*

Row 20: Rep row 8.

Row 21: Rep row 3, changing to D in last dc; cut C, turn. *(45 dc)*

Row 22: Rep row 4.

Row 23: Rep row 5, changing to A in last dc; cut D, turn. *(47 dc)*

Row 24: Rep row 6.

Row 25: Rep row 7, changing to B in last dc; cut A, turn. *(49 dc)*

For All Sizes

Note: Work rem rows in same color sequence.

Row 16 [20, 20, 22, 26]: Ch 1, sc in first dc; *ch 3, sk next 2 dc, sc in next dc; rep from * to last 2 dc and turning ch-3; ch 3, sk last 2 dc, sc in 3rd ch turning ch-3, turn.

Row 17 [21, 21, 23, 27]: Ch 3; *2 dc in next ch-3 sp; dc in next sc; rep from * across, changing to next color in last dc; cut old color, turn.

Rep last 2 rows until piece measures 9½ [11½, 14, 15, 17] inches from beg, ending with RS row.

Fasten off and weave in all ends.

Assembly

Sew shoulder seams to markers. Sew in Sleeves. Sew side and Sleeve seams.

Right Front Edging

Row 1 (RS): Hold Cardigan with RS facing you and Right Front edge at top; join A with sl st in end of row 1 of Right Front; ch 1, sc in same sp; working in ends of rows of Right Front, sc evenly spaced to top of Right Front, turn.

Row 2: Ch 1, working in **back lps** *(see page 28)* only, sc in each sc. Fasten off.

Left Front Edging

Row 1 (RS): Hold Cardigan with RS facing you and Left Front edge at top; join A with sl st in end of last row of Left Front; ch 1, sc in same sp; working in ends of rows of Left Front, sc evenly spaced to row 1, turn.

Row 2: Ch 1, working in back lps only, sc in each sc.

Fasten off and weave in all ends.

Finishing

Step 1: Fold upper corners of Fronts to form lapels. To secure lapels to Fronts, with sewing needle and matching thread, sew 1 button to corner of each lapel.

Step 2: Sew rem buttons to Left Front, having top button at beg of lapel shaping, bottom button 1 inch from lower edge, and rem button spaced evenly between.

A TOUCH OF RED

Designs by Edie Eckman

Skill Level

EASY

Sizes

Hat and Mittens: Instructions given fit child's size medium; changes for child's size large and adult's size are in [ ]. Scarf: Instructions given fit child's size; changes for adult's size are in [ ].

Finished Garment Measurements

Hat: 20 [21, 22] -inch circumference
Mittens: 6 [6½, 7] inches long with cuff
Scarf: 8 x 50 [10 x 58] inches

Materials

Hat and Mittens

- Medium (worsted) weight yarn:
  4 [4, 5] oz/280 [280, 350] yds/140 [140, 210]g white (A)
  4 [4, 5] oz/280 [280, 350] yds/140 [140, 210]g black (B)
  1 [1, 1] oz/70 [70, 70] yds/28 [28, 28]g red (C)
- Size H/8/5mm crochet hook or size needed to obtain gauge
- Tapestry needle
- Stitch marker

Scarf

- Medium (worsted) weight yarn:
  8 [9] oz/560 [630] yds/280 [315]g white (A)
  8 [9] oz/560 [630] yds/280 [315]g black (B)
  1 [1] oz/70 [70] yds/28 [28]g red (C)
- Size H/8/5mm crochet hook or size needed to obtain gauge
- Tapestry needle

Gauge

18 sc = 4 inches

Special Stitches

Front post triple crochet (fptr): Yo twice, insert hook from front to back to front around **post** (see page 28) of st indicated, draw lp through, [yo, draw through 2 lps on hook] 3 times.

Back post triple crochet (bptr): Yo twice, insert hook from back to front to back around **post** (see page 28) of st indicated, draw lp through, [yo, draw through 2 lps on hook] 3 times.

Pattern Note

To change colors at round joinings, insert hook in stitch indicated, yarn over with new color and draw through stitch and loop on hook. Carry unused color on wrong side.

HAT INSTRUCTIONS

Rnd 1 (RS): Starting at top with C, ch 4; join with sl st to form ring; ch 1, 8 sc in ring; join with sl st in first sc.

Rnd 2: Ch 1, 2 sc in same sc and in each rem sc; join with sl st in first sc. (16 sc)

Rnd 3: Ch 1, sc in same sc, 2 sc in next sc; [sc in next sc, 2 sc in next sc] 7 times; join with sl st in first sc. (24 sc)

Rnd 4: Ch 1, sc in same sc and in next sc, 2 sc in next sc; [sc in next 2 sc, 2 sc in next sc] 7 times; join with sl st in first sc. (32 sc)

Rnd 5: Ch 1, sc in same sc and in each rem sc; join with sl st in first sc.

Rnd 6: Ch 1, sc in same sc, 2 sc in next sc; [sc in next 3 sc, 2 sc in next sc] 7 times; sc in next 2 sc; join with sl st in first sc. (40 sc)

Rnd 7: Rep rnd 5, changing to B at end of rnd.

Rnd 8: Ch 1, sc in same sc, ch 1, sk next sc; *sc in next sc, ch 1, sk next sc; rep from * around; join with sl st in first sc.

Rnd 9: Ch 1, sc in same sc, ch 1, sc in next ch-1 sp, ch 1; *sc in next sc, ch 1, sc in next ch-1 sp; rep from * around; join with sl st in first sc, changing to A.

Rnd 10: Sl st in next ch-1 sp, ch 1, sc in same sp; ch 1; *sc in next ch-1 sp, ch 1; rep from * around; sk first sc; join with sl st in next ch-1 sp.

Rnd 11: Ch 1, sc in same sp; ch 1; *sc in next ch-1 sp, ch 1; rep from * around; sk first sc; join with sl st in next ch-1 sp, changing to B.

Rnd 12: Ch 1, sc in same sp; ch 1; *sc in next ch-1 sp, ch 1; rep from * around; sk first sc; join with sl st in next ch-1 sp.

Rnd 13: Rep rnd 11, changing to A at end of rnd.

Rnd 14: Rep rnd 12.

Rnd 15: Rep rnd 11, changing to B at end of rnd.

Rnd 16: Ch 1, sc in same sp; ch 1, [sc in next ch-1 sp, ch 1] 7 times; sc in next sc, ch 1; *[sc in next ch-1 sp, ch 1] 8 times; sc in next sc, ch 1; rep from * 3 times; join with sl st in first sc. (45 sc)

Rnd 17: Sl st in next ch-1 sp, ch 1, sc in same sp, ch 1; *sc in next ch-1 sp, ch 1; rep from * around; sk first sc; join with sl st in next ch-1 sp, changing to A.

Rnd 18: Ch 1, sc in same sp, ch 1; *sc in next ch-1 sp, ch 1; rep from * around; sk first sc; join with sl st in next ch-1 sp.

For Child's Size Medium Only

Continuing in stripe pattern as established, rep rnd 18 until piece measures 7¾ inches from beg, ending with a B row. Cut A. Continue with Ribbing.

For Child's Size Large & Adult's Size Only

Rnds 19–23: Continuing in stripe pattern as established, rep rnd 18.

Rnd 24: Ch 1, sc in same sp; ch 1; *[sc in next ch-1 sp, ch 1] 21 [10] times; sc in next sc, ch 1; rep from * 1 [3] times; sk first sc; join with sl st in next ch-1 sp.

Continuing in stripe pattern as established, rep rnd 18 until piece measures 8½ [9] inches from beg, ending with a B row. Cut A. Continue with Ribbing.

Ribbing

Rnd 1: Continuing with B, ch 3 (counts as a dc on this and following rnds), dc in each sc and in each ch-1 sp; join with sl st in 3rd ch of beg ch-3. (90 [94, 98] sc)

Rnd 2: Ch 3, **fptr** (see Special Stitches) around next dc; ***bptr** (see Special Stitches) around next dc; fpdc around next dc; rep from * around; join with sl st in 3rd ch of beg ch-3.

Rnd 3: Ch 3, fptr around next st; *bptr around next st; fptr around next st; rep from * around; join with sl st in 3rd ch of beg ch-3.

For Child's Size Medium Only

Fasten off and weave in all ends.

Fold up Ribbing.

For Child's Size Large & Adult's Size Only

Rnd 4: Rep rnd 3.

Fasten off and weave in all ends.

Fold up Ribbing.

MITTEN INSTRUCTIONS
Make 2.

Rnd 1: Starting at tip with C, ch 2; 5 sc in 2nd ch from hook; join with sl st in first sc.

Rnd 2: Ch 1, 2 sc in same sc and in each rem sc; join with sl st in first sc. (10 sc)

Rnd 3: Rep rnd 2. (20 sc at end of rnd)

For Child's Size Medium Only

Rnd 4: Ch 1, sc in same sc and in next sc; *2 sc in next sc; sc in next 2 sc; rep from * 5 times; join with sl st in first sc. (26 sc)

Rnd 5: Ch 1, sc in same sc and in each rem sc; join in first sc. Change to B by drawing lp through; cut A.

Continue with For All Sizes.

For Child's Size Large Only

Rnd 4: Ch 1, sc in same sc; 2 sc in next sc; *sc in next sc; 2 sc in next sc; rep from * 8 times; join with sl st in first sc. (30 sc)

Rnd 5: Ch 1, sc in same sc and in each rem sc; join in first sc. Change to B by drawing lp through; cut A.

Continue with For All Sizes.

For Adult's Size Only

Rnd 4: Ch 1, sc in same sc; 2 sc in next sc; *sc in next sc, 2 sc in next sc; rep from * 8 times; join with sl st in first sc. (30 sc)

Rnd 5: Ch 1, sc in same sc and in next sc; *2 sc in next sc; sc in next 6 sc; rep from * 3 times; join with sl st in first sc. (34 sc)

Change to B by drawing lp through; cut A.

Continue with For All Sizes.

For All Sizes

Rnd 6: Ch 1, sc in same sc; ch 1, sk next sc; *sc in next sc, ch 1, sk next sc; rep from * around; join with sl st in first sc.

Rnd 7: Sl st in next ch-1 sp, ch 1, sc in same sp; ch 1; *sc in next ch-1 sp, ch 1; rep from * around; sk first sc; join with sl st in next ch-1 sp, changing to B.

Rnd 8: Ch 1, sc in same sp; ch 1; *sc in next ch-1 sp, ch 1; rep from * around; sk first sc; join with sl st in next ch-1 sp.

Continuing in stripe pattern as established, rep rnd 8 until piece measures 4½ [5, 6] inches from beg, ending with a B rnd.

Thumb Opening

Note: Continue in stripe pattern.

Rnd 1: Ch 1, sc in same sp; [ch 1, sc in next ch-1 sp] 5 [6, 7] times; ch 7 [7, 9]; sk next 5 sts, [sc in next ch-1 sp, ch 1, sk next sc] 5 [6, 7] times; join with sl st in first ch-1 sp.

Rnd 2: Ch 1, sc in same sp; [ch 1, sc in next ch-1 sp] 4 [5, 6] times; ch 1, sk next sc, sc in next 7 [7, 9] chs; ch 1, [sc in next ch-1 sp, ch 1] 6 [7, 8] times; sk first sc; join with sl st in next ch-1 sp.

Rnd 3: Ch 1, sc in same sp; [ch 1, sc in next ch-1 sp] 4 [5, 6] times; [ch 1, sk next sc, sc in next sc] 3 [3, 4] times; ch 1, sk next sc, [sc in next ch-1 sp, ch 1] 5 [6, 7] times; sk first sc; join with sl st in next ch-1 sp.

Rnd 4: Ch 1, sc in same sp; ch 1; *sc in next ch-1 sp, ch 1, rep from * around; sk first sc; join with sl st in next ch-1 sp.

Rep rnd 4 until piece measures 1¼ [1½, 1¾] inches from Thumb Opening, ending with a B rnd.

Cuff

Rnd 1: Continuing with B, ch 1, sc in same sp; working in each sc and in each ch-1 sp, sc in next 3 [4, 7] sts, **sc dec** (see page 24) in next 2 sts; *sc in next 5 [6, 7] sts, sc dec in next 2 sts; rep from * twice; join with sl st in first sc. (23 [27, 33] sc)

Rnd 2: Ch 3 *(counts as a dc on this and following rnds)*, dc in each sc and in same sc as beg ch 3 made; join with sl st in 3rd ch of beg ch-3. *(24 [28, 34] dc)*

Rnd 3: Ch 3, **fptr** *(see Special Stitches)* around next dc; ***bptr** (see Special Stitches)* around next dc; fptr around next dc; rep from * 10 [12, 15] times; join with sl st in 3rd ch of beg ch-3.

Rnd 4: Rep rnd 3.

For Child's Size Medium Only

Fasten off.

Continue with Thumb.

For Child's Size Large & Adult's Size Only

Rnd 5: Rep rnd 3. Fasten off.

Continue with Thumb.

Thumb

Note: Thumb is worked in continuous rnds. Do not join; mark beg of rnds.

Rnd 1: Join B with sl st in first unused ch-1 sp of Thumb Opening; ch 1, sc in same sp and in next ch-1 sp; sc in side of next sc, in unused lps of next 7 [7, 9] chs, and in side of next sc. *(11 [11, 13] sc)*

Rnd 2: Sc in each sc.

Rnd 3: Sc in next 4 [4, 5] sc, sc dec in next 2 sc; sc in next 5 [5, 6] sc. *(10 [10, 12] sc)*

Rep rnd 2 until piece measures 1½ [2, 2¼] inches from beg.

Last rnd: [Sc dec] 5 [5, 6] times.

Fasten off, leaving an 8-inch end for sewing. Weave in other ends.

With tapestry needle, weave long end through rem sts and pull tightly. Secure end.

SCARF INSTRUCTIONS

Ribbing

Row 1: With B, ch 32 [40]; dc in 4th ch from hook *(beg 3 sk chs count as a dc)* and in each rem ch, turn. *(30 [38] dc)*

Row 2: Ch 3 (counts as a dc on this and following rows), ***fptr** (see Special Stitches)* around next dc; **bptr** *(see Special Stitches)* around next dc; rep from * 13 [17] times; dc in 3rd ch of beg 3 sk chs, turn.

Row 3: Ch 3; *fptr around next st; bptr around next st; rep from * 13 [17] times; dc in 3rd ch of turning ch-3, turn.

Row 4: Rep row 3.

For Child's Size Only

Continue with For All Sizes.

For Adult's Size Only

Row 5: Rep row 3.

Continue with For All Sizes.

For All Sizes

Row 5 [6]: Ch 1, sc in first 4 [5] dc, 2 sc in next dc; *sc in next 4 [5] dc, 2 sc in next dc; rep from * 3 times; sc in next 4 [7] dc and in 3rd ch of turning ch-3, turn. *(35 [43] sc)*

Body

Note: When changing color, draw up lp in last sc; draw new color through both lps on hook. Do not cut old color; carry unused color along edge of scrap.

Row 1: Ch 1, sc in first sc; *ch 1, sk next sc, sc in next sc; rep from * across, turn.

Row 2: Ch 1, sc in first sc and in next ch-1 sp; *ch 1, sc in next ch-1 sp; rep from * 14 [18] times; sc in next sc, changing to A, turn.

Row 3: Ch 1, sc in first sc and in next ch-1 sp; *ch 1, sc in next ch-1 sp; rep from * 14 [18] times; sc in next sc, turn.

Row 4: Rep row 3, changing to B in last sc.

Row 5: Rep row 3.

Rep rows 2–5 until piece measures approximately 38 [48] inches from beg, ending with a row 2. At end of last row, do not change to A. Fasten off A.

Ending Ribbing

Row 1: With B, ch 1, working in each sc and in each ch-1 sp, sc in first 4 [5] sts; ***sc dec** (see page 24) in next 2 sts; sc in next 4 [5] sts; rep from * 3 times; sc dec in next 2 sts; sc in next 5 [8] sts, turn. *(30 [38] sts)*

Row 2: Ch 3, dc in each rem sc, turn.

Row 3: Ch 3; *fptr around next dc; bptr around next dc; rep from * 13 [17] times; dc in 3rd ch of turning ch-3, turn.

Row 4: Ch 3, *fptr around next st; bptr around next st; rep from * 13 [17] times; dc in 3rd ch of turning ch-3, turn.

Row 5: Rep row 4.

For Child's Size Only

Fasten off and weave in ends.

Continue with Fringe.

For Adult's Size Only

Row 6: Rep row 4.

Continue with Fringe.

Fringe

Cut 8-inch strands of C. For each knot of fringe use 3 strands. Fold strands in half. Draw folded end through corner of 1 short end of Scarf. Draw ends through fold and tighten knot. Tie 7 [9] additional knots evenly spaced across end of Scarf. Tie 8 [10] knots evenly spaced across rem short end. Trim ends even.

SLEEPY-TIME BABY BLANKET

Skill Level

EASY

Finished Size

Approximately 31 x 36

Materials

- Fine (sport) weight yarn:
  8 oz/760 yds/224g
  white *(A)*
  4 oz/380 yds/112g yellow *(B)*
  3 oz/285 yds/84g pink *(C)*
  2 oz/190 yds/56g blue *(D)*
- Size G/6/4mm crochet hook or
  size needed to obtain gauge
- Tapestry needle

Gauge

4 sc = 1 inch

Pattern Note

To change colors, work until 2 loops
of last stitch remain on hook. With
new color, yarn over and draw through
2 loops on hook. Cut old color.

INSTRUCTIONS

Foundation row (WS): With B, ch 201
loosely; sc in 2nd ch from hook and in
next 4 chs, 3 sc in next ch; *sc in next 3
chs, sk next 2 chs, sc in next 3 chs, 3 sc in
next ch; rep from * to last 5 chs; sc in last
5 chs, turn.

Row 1 (RS): Ch 1, working in **back lps**
(see page 28) only, **sc dec** *(see page 24)* in
first 2 sc; sc in next 4 sts, 3 sc in next st;
*sc in next 3 sts, sk next 2 sts, sc in next
3 sts, 3 sc in next st; rep from * to last 6
sts; sc in next 4 sts, sc dec in last 2 sts,
changing to A in last st, turn.

Row 2: Ch 1, working in back lps only,
sc dec in first 2 sc; sc in next 4 sts, 3 sc in
next st; *sc in next 3 sts, sk next 2 sts, sc
in next 3 sts, 3 sc in next st; rep from * to
last 6 sts; sc in next 4 sts, sc dec in last 2
sts, turn.

Rep row 2 in following color sequence,
changing colors as necessary: 3 rows A, 2
rows C, 2 rows A, 2 rows C, 4 rows A, 2
rows B, 4 rows A, 4 rows D, 4 rows A, 8
rows B, 4 rows A, 4 rows D, 4 rows A, 2
rows B, 4 rows A, 2 rows C, 2 rows A, 2
rows C, 4 rows A, 2 rows B, 4 rows A, 4
rows D, 4 rows A, 8 rows B, 4 rows A, 4
rows D, 4 rows A, 2 rows B, 4 rows A, 2
rows C, 2 rows A, 2 rows C, 4 rows A, 2
rows B.

Fasten off and weave in all ends.

EXTRA CREDIT

Chapter 6

CLUSTERS & STRIPES

Design by Kelly Robinson

Skill Level

EASY

Finished Size

Approximately 45 x 60 inches

Materials

- Medium (worsted) weight yarn: 30 oz/2,100 yds/900g assorted scrap colors 15 oz/1,050 yds/450g off-white *(A)* 7½ oz/525 yds/225g black (B)
- Size H/8/5mm crochet hook or size needed to obtain gauge
- Tapestry needle

Gauge

4 dc = 1 inch

Special Stitch

Cluster (cl):

Keeping last lp of each dc on hook, 4 dc in st indicated; yo and draw through all 5 lps on hook.

Pattern Note

To change colors, work until 2 loops of last stitch remain on hook. With new color, yarn over and draw through 2 loops on hook. Cut old color.

INSTRUCTIONS

Row 1 (RS): With scrap color, ch 159; dc in 3rd ch from hook *(beg 2 sk chs count as a dc)* and in each rem ch, changing to B in last dc, turn.

Row 2: Ch 1, sc in first dc, in each rem dc and in 2nd ch of beg 2 sk chs, changing to new scrap color in last sc, turn.

Row 3: Ch 2 *(counts as a dc on this and following rows)*, sk first sc, dc in each rem sc, changing to A in last dc, turn.

Row 4: Ch 1, sc in first 2 dc; *cl *(see Special Stitch)* in next dc; sc in next 2 dc; rep from * to last 2 dc and turning ch-2; cl in next dc; sc in next dc and in 2nd ch of turning ch-2, changing to new scrap color in last sc, turn.

Row 5: Ch 2, sk first sc, dc in each rem sc and in each cl, changing to B in last dc, turn.

Row 6: Ch 1, sc in each dc and in 2nd ch of turning ch-2, changing to new scrap color in last dc, turn.

Rows 7–150: [Work rows 3–6] 36 times.

Row 151: Rep row 3. At end of row, do not change color.

Fasten off and weave in all ends.

POPCORN DIAMOND PILLOW

Design by Mary Ann Frits

Skill Level

EASY

Finished Size

Approximately 14 x 14 inches

Materials

- Red Heart Classic medium (worsted) weight yarn (3½ oz/190 yds/99g per skein): 3 skeins #3 off-white
- Size H/8/5mm crochet hook or size needed to obtain gauge
- Tapestry needle
- 14 x 14-inch pillow form

Gauge

Rnds 1–3 = 3 inches

Special Stitches

Popcorn (pc):

Ch 1, 5 dc in sp or st indicated; drop lp from hook, insert hook in ch 1, draw dropped lp through st on hook.

Beginning cluster (beg cl):

Ch 3, keeping last lp of each dc on hook, 2 dc in st indicated; yo and draw through all 3 lps on hook.

Cluster (cl):

Keeping last lp of each dc on hook, 3 dc in st indicated; yo and draw through all 4 lps on hook.

INSTRUCTIONS

Front

Rnd 1 (RS): Ch 8; join to form a ring; ch 3 *(counts as a dc on this and following rnds)*; *pc *(see Special Stitches)* in ring; dc in ring; rep from * 6 times; pc in ring; join with sl st in 3rd ch of beg ch-3. *(8 pc)*

Rnd 2: In same ch as joining work [**beg cl** *(see Special Stitches)*, ch 2, **cl** *(see Special Stitches)*]—*beg corner made*; *ch 1, sk next pc, 3 dc in next dc; ch 1, sk next pc, in next dc work (cl, ch 2, cl)—*corner made*; rep from * twice; ch 1, sk next pc, 3 dc in next dc, ch 1; join with sl st in beg cl.

Rnd 3: Sl st in next ch-2 sp; beg corner in same sp; *ch 1, 2 dc in next ch-1 sp; dc in next 3 dc, 2 dc in next ch-1 sp; ch 1, corner in ch-2 sp of next corner; rep from * twice; ch 1, 2 dc in next ch-1 sp; dc in next 3 dc, 2 dc in next ch-1 sp; ch 1; join with sl st in beg cl.

Rnd 4: Sl st in next ch-2 sp; beg corner in same sp; *ch 1, 2 dc in next ch-1 sp; dc in next 7 dc, 2 dc in next ch-1 sp; ch 1, corner in ch-2 sp of next corner; rep from * twice; ch 1, 2 dc in next ch-1 sp; dc in next 7 dc, 2 dc in next ch-1 sp; ch 1; join with sl st in beg cl.

Rnd 5: Sl st in next ch-2 sp; beg corner in same sp; *ch 1, 2 dc in next ch-1 sp; dc in next 5 dc, pc in next dc; dc in next 5 dc, 2 dc in next ch-1 sp; ch 1, corner in ch-2 sp of next corner; rep from * twice; ch 1, 2 dc in next ch-1 sp; dc in next 5 dc, pc in next dc; dc in next 5 dc, 2 dc in next ch-1 sp; ch 1; join with sl st in beg cl.

Rnd 6: Sl st in next ch-2 sp; beg corner in same sp; *ch 1, dc in next ch-1 sp; dc in next 5 dc, pc in next dc; dc in next dc, in ch in back of next pc and in next dc, pc in next dc; dc in next 5 dc, dc in next ch-1 sp; ch 1, corner in ch-2 sp of next

Back of pillow is shown.

corner; rep from * twice; ch 1, dc in next ch-1 sp; dc in next 5 dc, pc in next dc; dc in next dc, in ch in back of next pc and in next dc, pc in next dc; dc in next 5 dc, dc in next ch-1 sp; ch 1; join with sl st in beg cl.

Rnd 7: Sl st in next ch-2 sp; beg corner in same sp; *ch 1, 2 dc in next ch-1 sp; dc in next 4 dc, pc in next dc; [dc in next dc, in ch in back of next pc and in next dc, pc in next dc] twice; dc in next 4 dc, 2 dc in next ch-1 sp; ch 1, corner in ch-2 sp of next corner; rep from * twice; ch 1, 2 dc in next ch-1 sp; dc in next 4 dc, pc in next dc; [dc in next dc, in ch in back of next pc and in next dc, pc in next dc] twice; dc in next 4 dc, 2 dc in next ch-1 sp; ch 1; join with sl st in beg cl.

Rnd 8: Sl st in next ch-2 sp; beg corner in same sp; *ch 1, dc in next ch-1 sp, dc in next 4 dc, pc in next dc; [dc in next dc, in ch in back of next pc and in next dc, pc in next dc] 3 times; dc in next 4 dc, dc in next ch-1 sp, ch 1, corner in ch-2 sp of next corner; rep from * twice; ch 1, dc in next ch-1 sp, dc in next 4 dc, pc in next dc; [dc in next dc, in ch in back of next pc and in next dc, pc in next dc] 3 times; dc in next 4 dc, dc in next ch-1 sp, ch 1; join with sl st in beg cl.

Rnd 9: Sl st in next ch-2 sp; beg corner in same sp; *ch 1, 2 dc in next ch-1 sp; dc in next 3 dc, pc in next dc; [dc in next dc, in ch in back of next pc and in next dc, pc in next dc] 4 times; dc in next 3 dc, 2 dc in next ch-1 sp; ch 1, corner in ch-2 sp of next corner; rep from * twice; ch 1, 2 dc in next ch-1 sp; dc in next 3 dc, pc in next dc; [dc in next dc, in ch in back of next pc and in next dc, pc in next dc] 4 times; dc in next 3 dc, 2 dc in next ch-1 sp; ch 1; join with sl st in beg cl.

Rnd 10: Sl st in next ch-2 sp; beg corner in same sp; *ch 1, dc in next ch-1 sp, dc in next 3 dc, pc in next dc; [dc in next dc, in ch in back of next pc and in next dc, pc in next dc] 5 times; dc in next 3 dc, dc in next ch-1 sp, ch 1, corner in ch-2 sp of next corner; rep from * twice; ch 1, dc in next ch-1 sp, dc in next 3 dc, pc in next dc; [dc in next dc, in ch in back of next pc and in next dc, pc in next dc] 5 times; dc in next 3 dc, dc in next ch-1 sp, ch 1; join with sl st in beg cl.

Rnd 11: Sl st in next ch-2 sp; beg corner in same sp; *ch 1, 2 dc in next ch-1 sp; dc in next 2 dc, pc in next dc; [dc in next dc, in ch in back of next pc and in next dc, pc in next dc] 6 times; dc in next 2 dc, 2 dc in next ch-1 sp; ch 1, corner in ch-2 sp of next corner; rep from * twice; ch 1, 2 dc in next ch-1 sp; dc in next 2 dc, pc in next dc; [dc in next dc, in ch in back of next pc and in next dc, pc in next dc] 6 times; dc in next 2 dc, 2 dc in next ch-1 sp; ch 1; join with sl st in beg cl.

American School of Needlework, Berne, IN 46711 • ASNpub.com

Rnd 12: Sl st in next ch-2 sp; beg corner in same sp; *ch 1, dc in next ch-1 sp, dc in next 2 dc, pc in next dc; [dc in next dc, in ch in back of next pc and in next dc, pc in next dc] 7 times; dc in next 2 dc, dc in next ch-1 sp, ch 1, corner in ch-2 sp of next corner; rep from * twice; ch 1, dc in next ch-1 sp, dc in next 2 dc, pc in next dc; [dc in next dc, in ch in back of next pc and in next dc, pc in next dc] 7 times; dc in next 2 dc, dc in next ch-1 sp, ch 1; join with sl st in beg cl.

Rnd 13: Ch 3, 3 dc in next ch-2 sp; *dc in each cl, in each ch-1 sp and in each st to ch-2 sp of next corner; 3 dc in ch-2 sp of corner; rep from * twice; dc in each cl, in each ch-1 sp and in each st to beg ch-3; join in 3rd ch of beg ch-3.

Fasten off and weave in ends.

Back

Rnd 1 (RS): Ch 8; join to form a ring; ch 3 *(counts as a dc on this and following rnds)*; 15 dc in ring; join with sl st in 3rd ch of beg ch-3. *(16 dc)*

Rnd 2: In same ch as joining work [**beg cl** *(see Special Stitches)*, ch 2, **cl** *(see Special Stitches)*]—*beg corner made*; *ch 1, sk next dc, 3 dc in next dc; ch 1, sk next dc, in next dc work (cl, ch 2, cl)—*corner made*; rep from * twice; ch 1, sk next dc, 3 dc in next dc; ch 1; join with sl st in beg cl.

Rnd 3: Sl st in next ch-2 sp; beg corner in same sp; *ch 1, 2 dc in next ch-1 sp; dc in next 3 dc, 2 dc in next ch-1 sp; ch 1, corner in ch-2 sp of next corner; rep from * twice; ch 1, 2 dc in next ch-1 sp; dc in next 3 dc, 2 dc in next ch-1 sp; ch 1; join with sl st in beg cl.

Rnd 4: Sl st in next ch-2 sp; beg corner in same sp; *ch 1, 2 dc in next ch-1 sp; dc in next 7 dc, 2 dc in next ch-1 sp; ch 1, corner in ch-2 sp of next corner; rep from * twice; ch 1, 2 dc in next ch-1 sp; dc in next 7 dc, 2 dc in next ch-1 sp; ch 1; join with sl st in beg cl.

Rnd 5: Sl st in next ch-2 sp; beg corner in same sp; *ch 1, 2 dc in next ch-1 sp; dc in next 11 dc, 2 dc in next ch-1 sp; ch 1, corner in ch-2 sp of next corner; rep from * twice; ch 1, 2 dc in next ch-1 sp; dc in next 11 dc, 2 dc in next ch-1 sp; ch 1; join with sl st in beg cl.

Rnd 6: Sl st in next ch-2 sp; beg corner in same sp; *ch 1, dc in next ch-1 sp, dc in next 15 dc, dc in next ch-1 sp, ch 1, corner in ch-2 sp of next corner; rep from * twice; ch 1, dc in next ch-1 sp, dc in next 15 dc, dc in next ch-1 sp, ch 1; join with sl st in beg cl.

Rnd 7: Sl st in next ch-2 sp; beg corner in same sp; *ch 1, 2 dc in next ch-1 sp; dc in next 17 dc, 2 dc in next ch-1 sp; ch 1, corner in ch-2 sp of next corner; rep from * twice; ch 1, 2 dc in next ch-1 sp; dc in next 17 dc, 2 dc in next ch-1 sp; ch 1; join with sl st in beg cl.

Rnd 8: Sl st in next ch-2 sp; beg corner in same sp; *ch 1, dc in next ch-1 sp, dc in next 21 dc, dc in next ch-1 sp, ch 1, corner in ch-2 sp of next corner; rep from * twice; ch 1, dc in next ch-1 sp, dc in next 21 dc, dc in next ch-1 sp, ch 1; join with sl st in beg cl.

Rnd 9: Sl st in next ch-2 sp; beg corner in same sp; *ch 1, 2 dc in next ch-1 sp; dc in next 23 dc, 2 dc in next ch-1 sp; ch 1, corner in ch-2 sp of next corner; rep from * twice; ch 1, 2 dc in next ch-1 sp; dc in next 23 dc, 2 dc in next ch-1 sp; ch 1; join with sl st in beg cl.

Rnd 10: Sl st in next ch-2 sp; beg corner in same sp; *ch 1, dc in next ch-1 sp, dc in next 27 dc, dc in next ch-1 sp, ch 1, corner in ch-2 sp of next corner; rep from * twice; ch 1, dc in next ch-1 sp, dc in next 27 dc, dc in next ch-1 sp, ch 1; join with sl st in beg cl.

Rnd 11: Sl st in next ch-2 sp; beg corner in same sp; *ch 1, 2 dc in next ch-1 sp; dc in next 29 dc, 2 dc in next ch-1 sp; ch 1, corner in ch-2 sp of next corner; rep from * twice; ch 1, 2 dc in next ch-1 sp; dc in next 29 dc, 2 dc in next ch-1 sp; ch 1; join with sl st in beg cl.

Rnd 12: Sl st in next ch-2 sp; beg corner in same sp; *ch 1, dc in next ch-1 sp, dc in next 33 dc, dc in next ch-1 sp, ch 1, corner in ch-2 sp of next corner; rep from * twice; ch 1, dc in next ch-1 sp, dc in next 33 dc, dc in next ch-1 sp, ch 1; join with sl st in beg cl.

Rnd 13: Ch 3, 3 dc in next ch-2 sp; *dc in each ch-1 sp and in each dc to ch-2 sp of next corner; 3 dc in ch-2 sp of corner; rep from * twice; dc in each ch-1 sp and in each dc to beg ch-3; join in 3rd ch of beg ch-3.

Fasten off and weave in ends.

Border

Rnd 1 (RS): Hold Front and Back with WS tog; working through both pieces at same time, join yarn with sl st in any corner ch-3 sp; ch 3 *(counts as a dc)*; 2 dc in same sp; *dc in each st to next corner ch-3 sp; 3 dc in corner ch-3 sp; rep from * twice; insert pillow form; dc in each st to beg ch-3; join in 3rd ch of beg ch-3.

Rnd 2: Ch 1, sc in same ch as joining and in each dc; join in first sc.

Fasten off and weave in ends.

FLORAL CLUSTER SKIRT

Design by Svetlana Avrakh

Skill Level

EASY

Finished Sizes

Instructions given fit woman's X-small/small; changes for medium, large and X-large are in [ ].

Finished Garment Measurements

Hips: 36 inches *(X-small/small)* [39 inches *(medium)*, 42 inches *(large)*, 47 inches *(X-large)*]

Materials

- Bernat Cool Crochet light (light worsted) weight yarn (1¾ oz/200 yds/50g per ball): 4 [4, 5, 6] balls #74008 summer cream
- Size F/5/3.75mm crochet hook or size needed to obtain gauge
- Tapestry needle

Gauge

20 sc = 4 inches

Special Stitches

Half cluster (half cl):
Keeping last lp of each dc on hook, 3 dc in st indicated.

Cluster (cl):
Keeping last lp of each dc on hook, 3 dc in st indicated; yo and draw through all 4 lps on hook.

INSTRUCTIONS

Note: Skirt is worked from top down.

Front/Back
Make 2.

Row 1 (RS): Ch 121 [129, 137, 153]; sc in 2nd ch from hook; *ch 5, **half cl** *(see Special Stitches)* in 3rd ch from hook; sk next ch, half cl in next ch; sk next 3 chs, half cl in next ch; yo and draw through all 10 lps on hook—*half flower made*; ch 3, half cl in top of half flower just made; ch 3, sk next ch, sc in next ch; rep from * across, turn. *(15 [16, 17, 19] half flowers)*

Row 2: Ch 4, dc in next ch-3 sp; *ch 1, in top of next half flower work [**cl** *(see Special Stitches)*, ch 3, cl]; ch 1, **dc dec** *(see page 25)* in next 2 ch-3 sps; rep from * to last half flower; ch 1, in top of last half flower work (cl, ch 3, cl); ch 1, yo, draw up lp in sp formed by 3 sk chs of ch-5 sp, yo, draw through 2 lps on hook; yo twice, [yo, draw through 2 lps on hook] twice; yo and draw through all 3 lps on hook, turn.

Row 3: Ch 3, yo, draw up lp in first st, yo, draw through 2 lps on hook; half cl in top of next cl; yo and draw through all 3 lps on hook; *ch 3, half cl in top of st just made; ch 3, sc in next ch-3 sp, ch 5, half cl in 3rd ch from hook and in each of next 2 cls; yo and draw through all 10 lps on hook—*half flower made*; ch 3, cl in top of half flower just made; ch 3, sc in next ch-3 sp; rep from * across; ch 5, half cl in 3rd ch from hook and in next cl; yo, draw up lp in next dc; yo and draw through all 8 lps on hook, turn.

Row 4: Ch 4, cl in first st; *ch 1, dc dec in next 2 ch-3 sps; ch 1, in top of next half flower work (cl, ch 3, cl); rep from * sp formed by 3 sk chs of beg ch-5; ch 1, dc dec in sp formed by sk chs and next ch-3 sp; ch 1, in last st work (cl, ch 1, dc), turn.

Row 5: Ch 1, sc in first dc; *half flower over next 2 cls; ch 3, sc in next ch-3 sp; rep from * to last 2 cls; half flower over last 2 cls; ch 3, sc in 3rd ch of turning ch-4, turn.

Rep rows 2–5 until piece measures 24 inches or desired length from beg, ending with a WS row.

Fasten off and weave in ends.

Assembly
Sew side seams.

Waistband
Rnd 1: Hold piece with RS facing you and beg ch at top; join yarn with sl st in first ch-2 sp of beg ch; 2 sc in same sp; *3 sc in next ch-3 sp; sc in next 2 ch-1 sps; rep from * around; join with sl st in first sc.

Rnd 2: Ch 1, sc in same sc as joining and in each rem sc; join with sl st in first sc.

Rnds 3–5: Rep rnd 2.

Fasten off and weave in ends.

Drawstring
With 2 strands held tog, make a ch 58 inches long. Fasten off and weave in ends.

Finishing
Beg at center of Front, thread Drawstring through Waistband. Tie in bow at center front.

LEARN-TO-BEAD BELT

Design by Karen Whooley

Skill Level

EASY

Finished Size

Approximately 66 inches excluding fringe

Materials

- Lion Suede bulky (chunky) weight yarn (3 oz/111 yds/85g per ball): 1 ball #202 vineyard print
- Size I/9/5.5mm crochet hook or size needed to obtain gauge
- Tapestry needle
- Wooden beads from Westrim Crafts:
  15 large-hole 12mm beads
  36 standard 12mm beads

Gauge

5 dc = 1½ inches

Pattern Note

See Bead Crochet Lesson on page 21.

INSTRUCTIONS

Note: String 15 large-hole beads on yarn.

Row 1 (RS): Leaving a 7-inch end, ch 2; sc in 2nd ch from hook, turn.

Row 2: Ch 1, 3 sc in sc, turn. *(3 sc)*

Row 3: Ch 1, sc in each sc, turn.

Row 4: Ch 1, 2 sc in first sc; sc in next sc, 2 sc in last sc, turn. *(5 sc)*

Row 5: Ch 1, sc in each sc, turn.

Row 6: Ch 3 *(counts as a dc and a ch-1 sp on this and following rows)*, sk next sc, dc in next sc, ch 1, sk next sc, dc in last sc, turn. *(3 dc)*

Row 7: Ch 1, sc in first dc and in next ch-1 sp; slide bead up close to work, sc in next dc, in next ch-1 sp and in 3rd ch of turning ch-3; ch 3, turn.

Row 8: Ch 3, sk next sc, dc in next sc, ch 1, sk next sc, dc in last sc, ch 2, turn.

Row 9: Ch 2 *(counts as a dc on this and following rows)*, dc in each ch-1 sp, in each dc and in 3rd ch of turning ch-3, turn. *(5 dc)*

Row 10: Ch 2, dc in each rem dc, turn.

Row 11: Ch 2, dc in each rem dc, turn.

Rows 12–89: [Work rows 6–11] 13 times.

Rows 90–92: Rep rows 6–8.

Row 93: Ch 1, sc in each dc, in each ch-1 sp and in 3rd ch of turning ch-3, turn. *(5 sc)*

Row 94: Ch 1, sc in each sc, turn.

Row 95: Ch 1, **sc dec** *(see page 24)* in next 2 sc; sc in next sc, sc dec in last 2 dc, turn. *(3 sc)*

Row 96: Ch 1, sc in each sc, turn.

Row 97: Ch 1, draw up lp in each sc, yo and draw through all 4 lps on hook.

Fasten off, leaving a 7-inch end. Weave in other ends.

Fringe

Cut ten 14-inch strands of yarn. For each knot of fringe, hold 5 strands tog and fold in half. Draw folded end through point at 1 short end. Draw ends through fold and tighten knot. With rem strands, tie knot in point at other short end. Trim ends even.

Thread 4 standard beads on 3 random strands of each knot and knot to secure beads.

Thread 3 standard beads on 2 random strands of each knot and knot to secure.

BEADED PARTY COASTERS

Designs by Nazanin S. Fard

Skill Level

EASY

Finished Size

Approximately 5 x 5 inches

Materials

- Aunt Lydia's Fashion Crochet (150 yds per ball):
  1 ball #325 tangerine *(A)*
  1 ball #625 sage *(B)*
  1 ball #377 tan *(C)*
- Size E/4/3.5mm crochet hook or size needed to obtain gauge
- Tapestry needle
- Small glass crow beads (6mm, two 16-inch strands per package) from Fire Mountain Gems:
  75 red-gold #1829GB (for tangerine coaster)
  45 green #1826GB (for sage coaster)
- Glass tile beads (3mm, two 16-inch strands per package) from Fire Mountain Gems:
  99 amber #5020GB (for tan coaster)
- Beading needle

Gauge

6 sc = 1 inch

Pattern Note

See Bead Crochet Lesson on page 21.

INSTRUCTIONS

Tangerine Coaster

Note: With beading needle, string all red-gold beads on A.

Row 1: With A, ch 25; sc in 2nd ch from hook and in each rem ch, turn.

Row 2: Ch 1, sc in each sc, turn.

Rows 3–30: Rep row 2.

Border

Rnd 1: Ch 1, sc in every sc; working across next side in ends of rows, sc in each row; working across next side in unused lps of beg ch, sc in each lp; working across next side in ends of rows, sc in each row; join with sl st in first sc.

Rnd 2: Ch 1, sc in next sc, *slide 3 beads up, ch 1, sc in next 2 sc; rep from * around; join with sl st in first sc.

Fasten off and weave in ends.

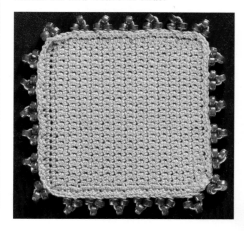

Sage Coaster

Note: With beading needle, string all green beads on B.

Row 1: With B, ch 27; dc in 4th ch from hook *(beg 3 sk chs count as a dc)*, dc in each rem ch, turn. *(25 dc)*

Row 2: Ch 1, sc in each dc and in 3rd ch of beg 3 sk chs, turn.

Row 3: Ch 3 *(count as a dc on this and following rows)*, dc in each rem sc, turn.

Row 4: Ch 1, sc in each dc and in 3rd ch of turning ch-3, turn.

Row 5: Ch 3, dc in each rem sc, turn.

Rows 6–17: [Work rows 4 and 5] 6 times.

Border

Rnd 1: Ch 1, sc in each dc and in 3rd ch of turning ch-3; working across next side in ends of rows, work 2 sc in end of each dc row and sc in end of each sc row; working across next side in unused lps of beg ch, sc in each lp; working across next side in ends of rows, work 2 sc in end of each dc row and sc in end of each sc row; join with sl st in first sc.

Rnd 2: Ch 1, *sc in next sc, slide 1 bead up, ch 1, sk next sc; rep from * around; join in first sc.

Fasten off and weave in ends.

Tan Coaster

Note: *With beading needle, string all amber beads on C.*

Row 1: With C, ch 27; sc in 2nd ch from hook and in each rem ch, turn. *(26 sc)*

Row 2: Ch 3 *(count as a dc on this and following rows)*, dc in next sc; *ch 1, sk next sc, dc in next 2 sc; rep from * across, turn.

Row 3: Ch 1, sc in each dc, in each ch-1 sp and in 3rd ch of turning ch-3, turn.

Rows 4–17: [Work rows 2 and 3] 7 times.

Border

Rnd 1: Ch 1, sc in each sc; working across next side in ends of rows, work 2 sc in end of each dc row and sc in end of each sc row; working across next side in unused lps of beg ch, sc in each lp; working across next side in ends of rows, work 2 sc in end of each dc row and sc in end of each sc row; join with sl st in first sc.

Rnd 2: Ch 1; * sc in next sc, slide 3 beads up, ch 1, sc in next sc, slide 1 bead up, ch 1; rep from * around; join with sl st in first sc.

Fasten off and weave in ends.

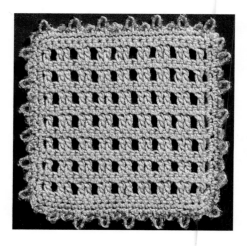

FELTED CATCH-ALL BOWL

Design by Zena Low

Skill Level

EASY

Finished Size

Approximately 9 inches in diameter x 5 inches high before felting
Approximately 5 inches in diameter x 4 inches high after felting (size will vary depending on amount of felting)

Materials

- Patons Classic Merino Wool medium (worsted) weight yarn (3½ oz/223 yds/100g per ball):
  1 ball #00205 deep olive *(A)*
  1 ball #00204 old gold *(B)*
  1 ball #00238 paprika *(C)*
- Size H/8/5mm crochet hook or size needed to obtain gauge
- Tapestry needle

Gauge

15 sc = 4 inches

INSTRUCTIONS

Base

Rnd 1 (RS): With A, ch 4; join with sl st to form ring; ch 1, 8 sc in ring; join with sl st in first sc. *(8 sc)*

Rnd 2: Ch 1, 2 sc in each sc; join with sl st in first sc. *(16 sc)*

Rnd 3: Ch 1, sc in same sc, 2 sc in next sc; [sc in next sc, 2 sc in next sc] 7 times; join with sl st in first sc. *(24 sc)*

Rnd 4: Ch 1, sc in same sc and in next sc, 2 sc in next sc; [sc in next 2 sc, 2 sc in next sc] 7 times; join with sl st in first sc. *(32 sc)*

Rnd 5: Ch 1, sc in same sc and in next 2 sc, 2 sc in next sc; [sc in next 3 sc, 2 sc in next sc] 7 times; join with sl st in first sc. *(40 sc)*

Rnd 6: Ch 1, sc in same sc and in next sc, 2 sc in next sc; [sc in next 4 sc, 2 sc in next sc] 7 times; sc in next 2 sc; join with sl st in first sc. *(48 sc)*

Rnd 7: Ch 1, sc in same sc and in each rem sc; join with sl st in first sc.

Rnd 8: Ch 1, sc in same sc and in next 4 sc, 2 sc in next sc; [sc in next 5 sc, 2 sc in next sc] 7 times; join with sl st in first sc. *(56 sc)*

Rnd 9: Ch 1, sc in same sc and in next 2 sc, 2 sc in next sc; [sc in next 6 sc, 2 sc in next sc] 7 times; sc in next 3 sc; join with sl st in first sc. *(64 sc)*

Rnd 10: Rep rnd 7.

Rnd 11: Ch 1, sc in same sc and in next 6 sc, 2 sc in next sc; [sc in next 7 sc, 2 sc in next sc] 7 times; join with sl st in first sc. *(72 sc)*

Rnd 12: Ch 1, sc in same sc and in next 3 sc, 2 sc in next sc; [sc in next 8 sc, 2 sc in next sc] 7 times; sc in next 4 sc; join with sl st in first sc. *(80 sc)*

Rnd 13: Rep rnd 7.

Rnd 14: Ch 1, sc in same sc and in next 8 sc, 2 sc in next sc; [sc in next 9 sc, 2 sc in next sc] 7 times; join with sl st in first sc. *(88 sc)*

Side

Rnds 15–17: Rep rnd 7.

Rnd 18: Ch 1, sc in same sc and in next 9 sc, 2 sc in next sc; [sc in next 10 sc, 2 sc in next sc] 7 times; join with sl st in first sc. *(96 sc)*

Fasten off.

Striped Section

Rnd 1: Join B with sl st in any sc; ch 1; sc in same sc, ch 1; *sc in next sc, ch 1; rep from * around; join with sl st in first sc. Fasten off.

Rnd 2: Join A with sl st in any ch-1 sp; ch 1, sc in same sp; ch 1, sk next sc; *sc in next ch-1 sp, ch 1, sk next sc; rep from * around; join with sl st in first sc.

Rnd 3: Sl st in next ch-1 sp; ch 1, sc in same sp; ch 1; sk next sc; *sc in next sc, ch 1, sk next sc; rep from * around; join with sl st in first sc. Fasten off.

Rnd 4: Join C with sl st in any sc; ch 1; sc in same sc, ch 1; *sc in next sc, ch 1; rep from * around; join with sl st in first sc. Fasten off.

Rnds 5 & 6: Rep rnds 2 and 3.

Rnds 7–18: [Work rnds 1–6] twice.

Rnds 19–21: Rep rnds 1–3. At end of rnd 21, do not fasten off.

Rnd 22: Sl st in next ch-1 sp; ch 1, sc in same sp; ch 1, sk next sc; *sc in next ch-1 sp, ch 1, sk next sc; rep from * around; join with sl st in first sc.

Rnd 23: Sl st in next ch-1 sp; ch 1, sc in same sp; ch 1; sk next sc; *sc in next sc, ch 1, sk next sc; rep from * around; join with sl st in first sc.

Edging

Ch 1, working from left to right, work reverse sc *(see page 27)* in same sc as joining, in each ch-1 sp and in each rem sc; join with sl st in first reverse sc.

Fasten off and weave in all ends.

FELTING

Felt piece as follows: Place piece in washing machine along with 1 tablespoon of detergent and a pair of jeans or other laundry. (Remember, do not wash crochet piece with other clothing that releases its own fibers.) Set washing machine on smallest load using hot water. Start machine and check progress after 10 minutes. Check progress more frequently after piece starts to felt. Reset machine if needed to continue agitation cycle. As piece becomes more felted, you may need to pull it into shape. When piece has felted to desired size, rinse it by hand in warm water. Remove excess water either by rolling in a towel and squeezing, or in the spin cycle of your washing machine. Block piece into shape, and let air dry. It may be helpful to stuff piece with a towel to help it hold its shape while drying.

FELTED BUSINESS TOTE

Design by Zena Low

Skill Level

EASY

Finished Size

Approximately 13 inches wide x 11 inches high before felting
Approximately 12 inches wide x 10 inches high after felting (size will vary depending on amount of felting)

Materials

- Patons Classic Merino Wool medium (worsted) weight yarn (3½ oz/223 yds/100g per ball): 3 balls #00226 black *(A)* 1 ball #00201 winter white *(B)*
- Sizes H/8/5mm and J/10/6mm crochet hooks or size needed to obtain gauge
- Tapestry needle

Gauge

Size H hook: 15 sc = 4 inches

INSTRUCTIONS

Front/Back

Make 2.

Foundation row (WS): With H hook and A, ch 50; sc in 2nd ch from hook and in each rem ch, turn. *(49 sc)*

Row 1 (RS): Ch 1, sc in each sc, turn.

Row 2: Ch 1, sc in each sc; change to B by drawing lp through; drop A, turn.

Row 3: Ch 1, sc in first sc; *ch 1, sk next sc, 3 dc in next sc; ch 1, sk next sc, sc in next sc; rep from * across. Fasten off.

Row 4 (RS): Hold piece with RS facing you; pick up A, ch 1, sc in first sc; *hdc in next sk sc on 2nd row below, on working row, sk next dc, sc in next dc, hdc in next sk sc on 2nd row below, on working row, sc in next sc; rep from * across, turn.

Note: *Push 3-dc groups to RS to form bobbles.*

Row 5: Ch 1, sc in each st; change to B by drawing lp through; drop A, turn.

Row 6: Ch 1, sc in first sc; *ch 1, sk next sc, sc in next sc, ch 1, sk next sc, 3 dc in next sc; rep from * to last 4 sc; [ch 1, sk next sc, sc in next sc] twice. Fasten off.

Row 7: Hold piece with RS facing you; pick up A, ch 1, sc in first sc, hdc in next sk sc on 2nd row below, on working row, sc in next sc, hdc in next sk sc in 2nd row below, sk next dc, sc in next dc, hdc in next sk sc on 2nd row below; rep from * to last 2 sts; sc in next sc, hdc in next sk sc on 2nd row below, sc in last sc, turn.

Note: Push 3-dc groups to RS to form bobbles.

Row 8: Ch 1, sc in each st; change to B by drawing lp through; drop A, turn.

Rows 9–56: [Work rows 3–8] 8 times.

Row 57: Ch 1, sc in each st.

Fasten off and weave in all ends.

Strap

Row 1: With J hook and 2 strands of A held tog, ch 7; sc in 2nd ch from hook and in each rem ch, turn. *(6 sc)*

Row 2: Ch 1, sc in each sc, turn.

Rep row 2 until piece measures 60 inches.

Fasten off and weave in ends.

FELTING

Felt pieces separately as follows: Place pieces in washing machine along with 1 tablespoon of detergent and a pair of jeans or other laundry. (Remember, do not wash crochet piece with other clothing that releases its own fibers.) Set washing machine on smallest load using hot water. Start machine and check progress after 10 minutes. Check progress more frequently after pieces start to felt. Reset machine if needed to continue agitation cycle. As pieces become more felted, you may need to pull them into shape. When pieces have felted to desired size, rinse them by hand in warm water. Remove excess water either by rolling in a towel and squeezing, or in the spin cycle of your washing machine. Block pieces into shape, and let air dry. It may be helpful to stuff piece with a towel to help it hold its shape while drying.

Assembly

With tapestry needle and A, sew ends of Strap tog. Sew Strap to Front, having seam at bottom of tote. Rep with Back.

BOTANICA PILLOWS

Design by Carol Wilson Mansfield

Skill Level

INTERMEDIATE

Finished Size

Approximately 14 x 14 inches

Materials

- Red Heart Super Saver medium (worsted) weight yarn (7 oz/364 yds/198g per skein):
  2 skeins #385 royal *(A)*
  1 skein #336 warm brown *(B)*
  1 skein #661 frosty green *(C)*
  1 skein #362 spruce *(D)*
  1 skein #316 soft white *(E)*
- Size H/8/5mm crochet hook or size needed to obtain gauge
- Tapestry needle
- 2 pillow forms, 14 x 14 inches

Gauge

4 dc = 1 inch
2 dc rows = 1 inch

Pattern Note

If you are unfamiliar with changing colors or working from a chart, refer to Changing Colors or Working From Charts on page 22.

INSTRUCTIONS

Pillow A

Front

Row 1 (RS): With A, ch 50; dc in 4th ch from hook *(beg 3 sk chs count as a dc)* and in each rem ch, turn. *(48 dc)*

Row 2: Ch 3 *(counts as a dc on this and following rows)*, dc in each rem dc and in 3rd ch of beg 3 sk chs, turn.

Row 3: Ch 3, dc in next 24 dc, changing to B in last dc; dc in next 2 dc, changing to A in last dc; dc in next 2 dc, changing to C in last dc; dc in next 8 dc, changing to A in last dc; dc in each rem dc and in 3rd ch of turning ch-3, turn.

Rows 4–28: Follow Pillow Chart A. At end of row 28, do not turn.

Edging

Ch 1, 3 sc in first dc—*corner made*; sc in each dc to turning ch-3; 3 sc in 3rd ch of turning ch-3—*corner made*; working across next side in ends of rows in sps formed by edge dc and turning chs, 2 sc in each row; working across next side in unused lps of beg ch, 3 sc in first lp—*corner made*; sc in each lp to last lp; 3 sc in last lp—*corner made;* working across next side in ends of rows in sps formed by edge dc and turning chs, 2 sc in each row; join with sl st in first sc.

Fasten off and weave in all ends.

Back

Row 1 (RS): With A, ch 50; dc in 4th ch from hook *(beg 3 sk chs count as a dc)* and in each rem ch, turn. *(48 dc)*

Row 2: Ch 3 *(counts as a dc on this and following rows)*, dc in each rem dc and in 3rd ch of beg 3 sk chs, turn.

Row 3: Ch 3, dc in each rem dc and in 3rd ch of turning ch-3, turn.

Rows 4–28: Rep row 3. At end of row 28, do not turn.

Edging

Work same as Edging for Front.

Assembly

With A, sew Front and Back tog along 3 sides. Insert pillow form. Sew rem side.

Pillow B

Front

Row 1 (RS): With A, ch 50; dc in 4th ch from hook *(beg 3 sk chs count as a dc)* and in each rem ch, turn. *(48 dc)*

Row 2: Ch 3 *(counts as a dc on this and following rows)*, dc in each rem dc and in 3rd ch of beg 3 sk chs, turn.

Row 3: Ch 3, dc in next 7 dc, changing to C in last dc; dc in next 7 dc, changing to A in last dc; dc in next 4 dc, changing to B in last dc; dc in next 2 dc, changing to A in last dc; dc in next 2 dc, changing to D in last dc; dc in next 2 dc, changing to C in last dc; dc in next 3 dc, changing to A in last dc; dc in next 2 dc, changing to C in last dc; dc in next 4 dc, changing to A in last dc; dc in each rem dc and in 3rd ch of turning ch-3, turn.

Rows 4–28: Follow Pillow Chart B. At end of row 28, do not turn.

Edging

Work same as Edging for Front of Pillow A.

Back

Work same as Back for Pillow A.

Assembly

Follow Assembly instructions for Pillow A.

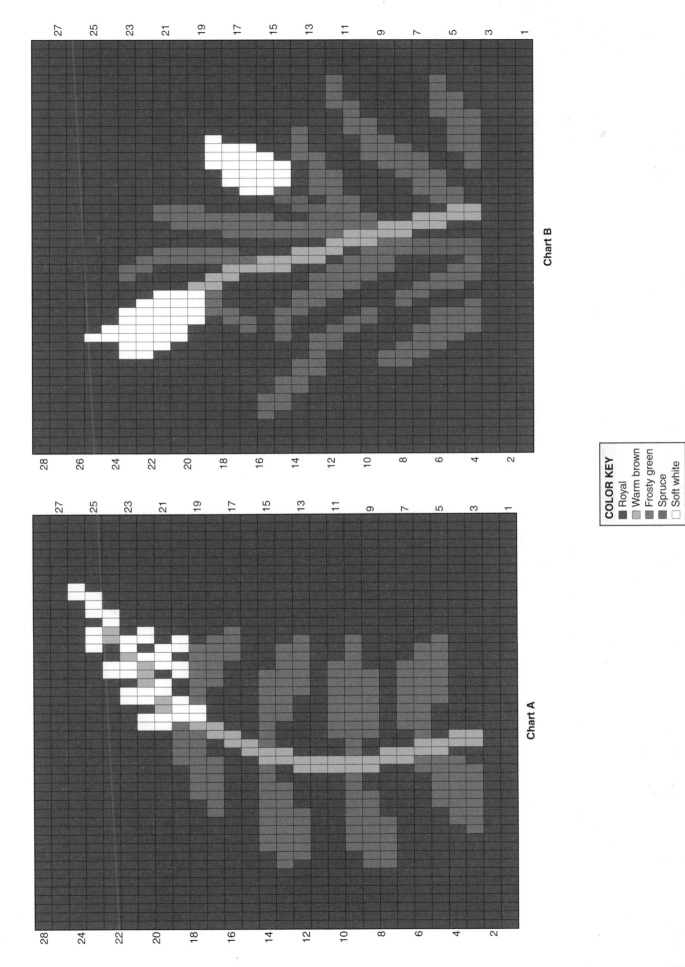

Chart A

Chart B

COLOR KEY
- Royal
- Warm brown
- Frosty green
- Spruce
- Soft white

SUNSHINE TOTE

Design by Carol Wilson Mansfield

Skill Level

INTERMEDIATE

Finished Size

Approximately 11 x 13 inches

Materials

- Red Heart Super Saver medium (worsted) weight yarn (7 oz/364 yds/198g per skein):
  1 skein #376 burgundy *(A)*
  1 skein #321 gold *(B)*
  1 skein #320 cornmeal *(C)*
- Red Heart Classic medium (worsted) weight yarn (3½ oz/190 yds/99g per skein):
  1 skein #252 medium coral *(D)*
- Size H/8/5mm crochet hook or size needed to obtain gauge
- Tapestry needle

Gauge

4 dc = 1 inch
2 dc rows = 1 inch

Pattern Note

If you are unfamiliar with changing colors or working from a chart, refer to Changing Colors or Working From Charts on page 22.

INSTRUCTIONS

Front/Back
Make 2.

Row 1 (RS): With A, ch 50; dc in 4th ch from hook *(beg 3 sk chs count as a dc)* and in each rem ch, turn. *(48 dc)*

Row 2: Ch 3 *(counts as a dc on this and following rows)*, dc in each rem dc and in 3rd ch of beg 3 sk chs, turn.

Row 3: Ch 3, dc in next 21 dc, changing to B in last dc; dc in next 4 dc, changing to A in last dc; dc in next 21 dc and in 3rd ch of turning ch-3, turn.

Rows 4–24: Follow chart; at end of row 24, do not turn.

Fasten off and weave in all ends.

Finishing

Step 1: Hold pieces with RS tog. With A, sew sides and bottom of pieces tog, leaving top edge open.

Step 2: For braided strap, cut six 3-yd strands each of A, B and D. Using all strands, braid to length of 45 inches, leaving 10 inches at each end unbraided.

Step 3: With A, tack braid to each side seam of tote leaving unbraided ends to form a tassel at each corner and 23 inches unattached at top to form strap.

COLOR KEY	
■	Burgundy
▨	Gold
☐	Cornmeal
▦	Coral

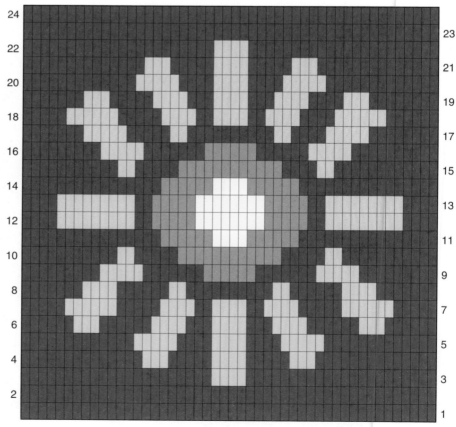

Sunshine Tote

SWEET WILLIAM

Design by Delsie Rhoades

Skill Level

EASY

Finished Size

Approximately 1½ inches wide by desired length (1 rep is approximately 1 inch long)

Materials

- Aunt Lydia's Classic Crochet bedspread weight crochet cotton (350 yds per ball):
  1 ball #495 wood violet *(A)*
  1 ball #420 cream *(B)*
- Size 5/1.90mm steel crochet hook or size needed to obtain gauge
- Tapestry needle

Note: 1 rep requires approximately 2 yds of A and 3 yds of B.

Gauge

8 dc = 1 inch

INSTRUCTIONS

Flower

Note: *Make 1 Flower for each inch of length desired.*

With A, ch 4; in 4th ch from hook work (dc, ch 3, sl st)—*petal made*; *ch 3, in same ch work (dc, ch 3, sl st)—*petal made*; rep from * 3 times. *(5 petals)*

Fasten off and weave in ends.

Edging

Row 1 (RS): Join B with sl st in dc of any petal; *[ch 5, sl st in dc of next petal] twice; holding WS of next Flower facing WS of working Flower, sl st in dc of any petal on next Flower; open flat and continue on RS; rep from * until all Flowers are joined; [ch 5, sl st in dc of next petal] twice, turn.

Row 2: Sl st in next ch-5 sp, ch 1, sc in same sp; *ch 5, sc in next ch-5 sp; rep from * across, turn.

Row 3: Sl st in next ch-5 sp, ch 1, sc in same sp; [ch 3, sc in same sp] 3 times; *sc in next ch-5 sp, [ch 3, sc in same sp] 3 times; rep from * across.

Fasten off and weave in ends.

MARIGOLD

Design by Delsie Rhoades

Skill Level

EASY

Finished Size

Approximately 1½ inches wide by desired length (1 rep is approximately 1½ inches long)

Materials

- Aunt Lydia's Classic Crochet bedspread weight crochet cotton (350 yds per ball):
  1 ball #131 fudge brown *(A)*
  1 ball #421 goldenrod *(B)*
  1 ball #419 ecru *(C)*
- Size 5/1.90mm steel crochet hook or size needed to obtain gauge
- Tapestry needle

Note: *1 rep requires approximately 2 yds of A and B and 5 yds of C.*

Gauge

8 dc = 1 inch

INSTRUCTIONS

Flower

Note: *Make 1 Flower for each 1½ inches of length desired.*

Rnd 1 (RS): With A, ch 2; 6 sc in 2nd ch from hook; join with sl st in first sc.

Rnd 2: Ch 1, 2 sc in same sc as joining and in each rem sc; join with sl st in first sc; change to B by drawing lp through. *(12 sc)*

Rnd 3: Ch 1, sc in same sc as joining; ch 3; *sc in next sc, ch 3; rep from * around; join with sl st in first sc.

Fasten off and weave in all ends.

Edging

Row 1 (WS): Hold 1 Flower with WS facing you; join C with sl st in any sc; ch 12 *(counts as a dc and a ch-9 sp)*, sk next 2 sc, in next sc work (sc, ch 3, sc); ch 9, sk next 2 sc, dc in next sc; *hold next Flower with WS facing you; dc in any sc of Flower, ch 9, sk next 2 sc, in next sc work (sc, ch 3, sc); ch 9, sk next 2 sc, dc in next sc; rep from * until all Flowers have been joined, turn.

Row 2 (RS): Sl st in next ch-9 sp, ch 1, 5 sc in same sp; *in next ch-3 sp work (dc, ch 4, sl st in 3rd ch from hook—*picot made*; ch 1, dc)—*shell made*; 5 sc in each of next 2 ch-9 sps; rep from * to last ch-3 sp and last ch-9 sp; shell in next ch-3 sp; 5 sc in last ch-9 sp.

Fasten off and weave in ends.

American School of Needlework, Berne, IN 46711 • ASNpub.com

DRG Publishing
306 East Parr Road
Berne, IN 46711
©2006 American School of Needlework

TOLL-FREE ORDER LINE or to request a free catalog (800) 582-6643
Customer Service (800) 282-6643, **Fax** (800) 882-6643

Visit AnniesAttic.com.

We have made every effort to ensure the accuracy and completeness of these instructions.
We cannot, however, be responsible for human error, typographical mistakes or variations in individual work.

ISBN: 978-1-59012-174-0
Printed in USA

7 8 9